ISBN 978-1-331-66617-2
PIBN 10059837

This book is a reproduction of an important historical work. Forgotten Books uses state-of-the-art technology to digitally reconstruct the work, preserving the original format whilst repairing imperfections present in the aged copy. In rare cases, an imperfection in the original, such as a blemish or missing page, may be replicated in our edition. We do, however, repair the vast majority of imperfections successfully; any imperfections that remain are intentionally left to preserve the state of such historical works.

QH81
P83m

"Thou art only a gray and sober dove,
But thine eye is faith and thy wing is love."
Lanier.

Books by

Gene Stratton-Porter

What I Have Done With Birds
At the Foot of the Rainbow
A Girl of the Limberlost
The Song of the Cardinal
The Music of the Wild.
Birds of the Bible
Freckles

Contents

PART I

List of Illustrations

List of Illustrations

12

List of Illustrations

13

List of Illustrations

14

List of Illustrations

To

Miles Fuller Porter

PART I

The Chorus of the Forest

"*I thought the sparrow's note from heaven,*
    Singing at dawn on the alder bough ;
I brought him home, in his nest, at even ;
    He sings the song, but it pleases not now,
For I did not bring home the river and sky ;
He sang to my ear,—they sang to my eye."
                                    —*Emerson.*

THE FOREST

"I know where wild things lurk and linger,
In groves as gray and grand as Time;
I know where God has written poems
Too strong for words or rhyme."
—Thompson.

THE PRIMARY MUSIC CLASS

The Chorus of the Forest

SINCE the beginning the forest has been singing its song, but few there are who have cared to learn either the words or the Forest Notes melody. Its chorus differs from that of any other part of the music of nature, and the price that must be paid to learn it is higher. The forest is of such gloomy and forbidding aspect that intimate acquaintance is required in order to learn to love it truly. So only a few peculiar souls, caring for solitude and far places, and oblivious to bodily discomfort, have answered this wildest of calls, and gone to the great song carnival among the trees.

The forest always has been compared rightly with a place of worship. Its mighty trees, sometimes appearing as if set in aisles, resemble large pillars, and the canopy formed by their overarching branches provides the subdued light conducive to worship. The dank, pungent air arises

Music of the Wild

as incense around you. Sunlight, streaming in white shafts through small interstices, suggests candles. Altars are everywhere, carpeted with velvet mosses, embroidered with lichens, and decorated with pale-faced flowers, the eternal symbol of purity and holiness. Its winds forced among overlapping branches sing softly as harps, roar and wail as great organs, and scream and sob as psalters and hautboys. Its insect, bird, and animal life has been cradled to this strange music until voices partake of its tones, so that they harmonize with their tree accompaniment, and all unite in one mighty volume, to create the chorus of the forest.

I doubt if any one can enter a temple of worship and not be touched with its import. Neither can one go to primal forests and not feel closer the spirit and essence of the Almighty than anywhere else in nature. In fact, God is in every form of creation; but in the fields and marshes the work of man so has effaced original conditions that he seems to dominate. The forest alone raises a chorus of praise under natural conditions. Here you can meet the Creator face to face, if anywhere on earth. Yet very few come to make His acquaintance.

The reason lies in the discomfort; the gloomy, forbidding surroundings. It may be that there yet lingers in the hearts of us a touch of that fear

THE ROAD TO THE FOREST

"And the wide forest weaves,
To welcome back its la l t ain

The Chorus of the Forest

inherited from days when most of the beasts and many of the birds were larger and of greater strength than man, so that existence was a daily battle. Then the forest is ever receding. As we approach, it retreats, until of late years it has become difficult to find, and soon it is threatened with extinction. As yet, it is somewhere, but patience and travel are required to reach it. I found the forest here pictured after a journey by rail, water, and a long road so narrow that it seemed as if every one traveling it went in the morning and returned at night, but none ever passed on the way.

Such a narrow little road, and so sandy that it appeared like a white ribbon stretched up gentle hill and down valley! On each side I saw evidence that lately it had been forest itself; else the way would not have been so very narrow, the sides impassable, and bordered with trees so mighty and closely set as to dwarf it to the vanishing point long within the range of vision. The very flowers were unusual, the faint musky perfume creeping out to us, a touch of the forest greeting our approach. The road ran long and straight, and where it ended the work of man ceased and the work of nature began. *The Road to the Forest*

The forest was surrounded by a garden, where sunlight and warmth encouraged a growth not to be found inside. Here in early spring daintiest

27

Music of the Wild

flowers had flourished: anemones and violets. Bloodroot had lifted bloom waxen-pure and white, and its exquisitely cut and veined slivery, blue-green leaves, set on pink coral stems, were yet thrifty. Now there were flowers, fruits, berries, and nuts in a profusion the fields never know, and with few except the insects, birds, butterflies, and squirrels to feast upon them. You could produce a rain of luscious big blackberries by shaking a branch.

The Forest Fence There were traces of a straggling snake-fence in one place, on top of which the squirrels romped and played. This could not have extended far, because the impenetrable swamp that soon met the forest stretched from sight.

Then the Almighty made the work of man unnecessary by inclosing the forest in a fence of His design, vastly to my liking. First was found a tangle of shrubs that wanted their feet in the damp earth and their heads in the light. Beneath them I stopped to picture tall, blue bellflower, late blue-bells, and spiderwort, with its peculiar leafage and bloom. There was the flame of foxfire, the lavender and purple of Joe-Pye weed, ironwort, and asters just beginning to show color, for it was middle August, and late summer bloom met early fall. There were masses of yellow made up of golden-rod beginning to open, marigold, yellow daisies, and cone-flowers.

BLOOD-ROOT

It has blood in its root and a waxen white face,
Coral stems and silver leaves of wonderful grace.

The Chorus of the Forest

But the real fence inclosing the forest was a hedge of dogwood, spicebrush, haw, hazel, scrub oak, maple, and elm bushes. At bloom time it must have been outlined in snowy flowers; now nuts and berries were growing, and all were interlaced and made impenetrable by woodbine. wildgrape, clematis, and other stoutly growing vines.

At first we could not see the gateway, but after a little searching it was discovered. Once found, it lay clear and open to all. The posts were slender, mastlike trunks shooting skyward; outside deep golden sunshine you almost thought you could handle as fabric, inside merely a few steps to forest darkness. Near the gateway a tiny tree was waging its battle to reach the sky, and a little farther a dead one was compelled to decay leaning against its fellows, for they were so numerous it could not find space to lie down and rest in peace. This explained at once that there would be no logs. All the trees would lodge in falling, and decay in that position, and their bark and fiber would help to make uncertain walking. **The Gateway**

At the gate is the place to pause and consider. The forest issues an universal invitation, but few there be who are happy in accepting its hospitality. If you carry a timid heart take it to the fields, where you can see your path before you and familiar sounds fall on your ears. If you carry a sad heart the forest is not for you. Nature places

31

Music of the Wild

gloom in its depths, sobs among its branches, cries from its inhabitants. If your heart is blackened with ugly secrets, better bleach them in the healing sunshine of the fields. The soul with a secret is always afraid, and fear was born and has established its hiding place in the forest. You must ignore much personal discomfort and be sure you are free from sadness and fear before you can be at home in the forest.

But to all brave, happy hearts I should say, "Go and learn the mighty chorus." Somewhere in *The Creator's Gift to Men* the depths of the forest you will meet the Creator. The place is the culmination of His plan for men adown the ages, a material thing proving how His work evolves, His real gift to us remaining in natural form. The fields epitomize man. They lay as he made them. They are artificial. They came into existence through the destruction of the forest and the change of natural conditions. They prove how man utilized the gift God gave to him. But in the forest the Almighty is yet housed in His handiwork and lives in His creation.

Therefore step out boldly. You are with the Infinite. Earth that bears trees from ten to fourteen feet in circumference, from forty to sixty to the branching, and set almost touching each other, will not allow you to sink far. You are in little danger of meeting anything that is not more frightened at your intrusion than you are at it:

THE GATEWAY

"To that cathedral, boundless as our wonder,
  Whose quenchless lamps the sun and moon supply;

The Chorus of the Forest

Cutting your path before you means clearing it of living things as well as removing the thicket of undergrowth. A hundred little creatures are fleeing at your every step, and wherever you set foot you kill without your knowledge; for earth, leaves, and mosses are teeming with life. You need only press your ear to the ground and lie still to learn that a volume of sound is rising to heaven from the creeping, crawling, voiceless creatures of earth, the minor tone of all its music.

The only way to love the forest is to live in it until you have learned its pathless travel, growth, and inhabitants as you know the fields. You must begin at the gate and find your road slowly, else you will not hear the Great Secret and see the Compelling Vision. There are trees you never before have seen; flowers and vines the botanists fail to mention; such music as your ears can not hear elsewhere, and never-ending pictures no artist can reproduce with pencil or brush.

This forest in the summer of 1907 was a complete jungle. The extremely late spring had delayed all vegetation, and then the prolonged and frequent rains fell during summer heat, forcing everything to unnatural size. Jewel-weed that we were accustomed to see attain a height of two feet along the open road, raised there that season to four, and in the shade of the forest overgrew a tall man; its pale yellow-green stems were like

35

Music of the Wild

bushes, and its creamy cornucopias dangled the size of foxglove, freckled with much paler brown than in strong light. The white violets were as large as their cultivated blue relatives, and nodded from stems over a foot in length. Possibly it was because they formed such a small spot of color in that dark place, possibly they were of purer white than flowers of larger growth in stronger light; no matter what the reason, these deep forest violets were the coldest, snowiest white of any flower I ever have seen. They made arrow-head lilies appear pearl white and daisies cream white compared with them.

Thinking of this caused me to notice the range of green colors also. The leaves and mosses near earth were the darkest, growing lighter through ferns, vines, bushes, and different tree leaves in never-ending shades. No one could have enumerated all of them. They were more variable and much more numerous than the grays. But in dim forest half-light all color appeared a shade paler than in mere woods.

From the all-encompassing volume of sound I endeavored to distinguish the instruments from the performers. The water, the winds, and the trees combined in a rising and falling accompaniment that never ceased. The insects, birds, and animals were the soloists, most of them singing, while some were performing on instruments. Always there

The Tree Harps

36

THE TREE HARPS

Knee-deep in the pungent forest,
God's Great Secret you may hear;
While to eyes of eager longing,
The Compelling Vision shines out clear.

The Chorus of the Forest

was the music of my own heart over some wondrous flower or landscape picture, or stirred to join in the chorus around me. The trees were large wind-harps, the trunks the framework, the branches the strings. These trunks always were wrapped in gray, but with each tree a differing shade. There were brown-gray, green-gray, blue-gray, dark-gray, light-gray, every imaginable gray, and many of them so vine-entwined and lichen-decorated it was difficult to tell exactly what color they were.

The hickory was the tatterdemalion; no other tree was so rough and ragged in its covering. Oak, elm, walnut, and ash, while deeply indented with the breaks of growth, had more even surface. The poplar, birch, and sycamore had the smoothest bark and showed the most color. The tall, straight birch did gleam "like silver," but to me the sycamore was more beautiful. The largest were of amazing size, whole branches a cream-white with big patches of green, and the rough bark of the trunks was a dirty yellow-gray. These trees always show most color in winter, but I do not know whether they really are brighter then, or whether the absence of the green leaves makes them appear so. Anywhere near the river the trees grew larger, and their uplifted branches caught the air and made louder music, while the unceasing song of the water played a minor accompaniment. These big wind-harps were standing

39

so close I could focus six of them, the least large
enough to be considered unusual in broken wood,
on one small photographic plate. Where several
sprang from a common base some of them were
forced to lean, but the great average grew skyward
straight as pines, and in the stillest hour the wind
whispered among the interlaced branches, and in a
gale roared to drown the voice of the thunder.

Little trees beginning their upward struggle to
reach the light caused me to feel that they were
destroying pictures of great beauty. At last we
found an elevation of some height and climbing
it, secured the view that awaited us. As soon as
we were level with the top of the undergrowth,
that was a tangle in the most open spaces, not
so dense where the trees grew closer together, it
appeared to stretch away endlessly, making a vari-
egated, mossy, green floor that at a little distance
seemed sufficiently material to bear our weight.
Knowing this to be an illusion, I sent my soul jour-
neying, instead. Crowding everywhere arose the
big, vine-entwined tree trunks, stretching from
forty to seventy feet to their branching. The cool
air of this enclosed space between the bush tops
and the tree branches had a spicy fragrance. The
carpet of green velvet below and the roof of green
branches above formed a dominant emerald note;
but it was mellowed with the soft grays of the tree
trunks and tinted with the penetrant blue of the

The Abid-
ing Place
of the Al-
mighty

40

THE GLOVES THE FOXES WEAR

"Nestled at this root
Is beauty, such as blooms not in the glare
Of the broad sun."
—Bryant.

The Chorus of the Forest

sky, so that the whole was a soft, blue-gray green, the most exquisite sight imaginable. All thought of the world outside vanished. The heart flooded with awe, adoration, and a great and holy peace. Here is the world's most beautiful Cathedral, where the unsurpassed tree-harps accompany the singers in nature's grandest anthem. This is the abiding-place of the Almighty in the forest.

When we dared linger no longer and attempted to reach certain trees superb above their fellows, we found that a path must be cut before us for long distances, and then at times, for no apparent reason, we came into open spaces underfoot and thinner branching overhead. These were brown and gray-carpeted with the heaped dead leaves of many seasons, and glorified with flower color, but there were no grasses. It was in places such as these that the joy song of the human heart drowned all other music. On the rich brown floor, against the misty gray-green background, flashed the pale yellow of false foxglove, the loveliest and the typical flower of the forest.

The tall, smooth stems were high as my head, the leaves sparse and tender, the bloom large and profuse, and of warm shades of light-yellow impossible to describe, because they vary with age. The buds are a pure warm yellow, the flower cowslip color on the first day, creamy white on the second, the fallen blooms showering the dark floor

The Gloves the Foxes Wear

43

almost white. These are the gloves the foxes wear when they travel the forest softly. Cultivated relatives of the family are not nearly so beautiful as the wild species.

I think this is true of the wild flowers, vines, and plants everywhere. Their hothouse relatives do not compare with them. Field and forest flowers are of more delicate color, they are simple and natural, and there is a touch of pure wildness in them akin to a streak in every heart. Of late people have been realizing this, and they have made efforts, not always agreeable to the plants, to remove and set them around houses and in gardens. Such flowers usually die a lingering death because they can not survive out of their element. The foxglove enters a more vigorous protest than any. It is as if the old mother of the family feared that when we saw her glorious shade-children we would steal them from their damp, dark home; and so, with the cunning of her namesakes, the foxes, she taught all her family to reach down and find the roots of surrounding trees, twine around them, and grow fast, until they became veritable parasites and not only clung for protection, but to suck life, so that they quickly withered and died if torn away. The effort to transplant foxglove always reminds me of an attempt to remove old people who have lived long on one spot and sent the roots of their affections clinging around things they

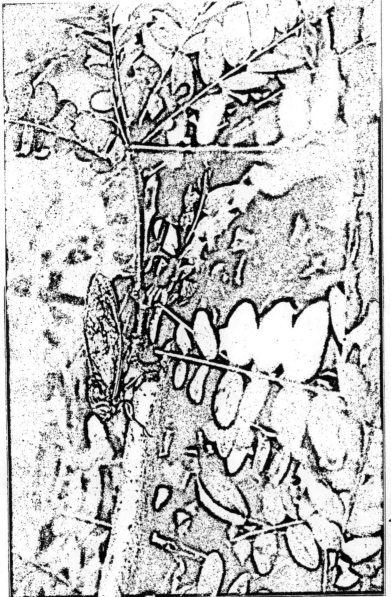

THE LOCUST'S FIDDLE

The locust fiddles on his shining wings,
The very same song that every bird sings,
Chants of praise for the life they know,
Notes of ten thousand years ago.

The Chorus of the Forest

love. Then some change comes, and an effort is made to remove them to a different location and atmosphere. They end the same as deep forest flowers brought into the strong light of yard and garden; only as a rule people pine and die more quickly.

A few bees humming around the foxglove set me to watching for insect musicians. The pale flowers of deep forest were not attractive as was The Locust's Fiddle the growth outside. There was only an occasional butterfly. But there were millions of other insects singing everywhere around us, and the leaders were the locusts. Sometimes they flew so close, making music on wing, that we dodged and our ears rang. We caught several and examined them, and induced one to pose for us on a locust tree. They are an inch and a half in length, a rare green color with brown markings, and have large eyes, a stout, sharp tongue, silvery white legs, and long wing-shields, appearing as if cut from thinnest isinglass, the shorter true wing beneath.

These wingshields are divided into small sections by veins that hold the transparent parts securely, and the outer edge has a stout rim. Using these rims for their strings, the crisp space for sounding-boards, and the femur of the hind legs for bows, the locust amazed us by not singing at all, for he fiddled away gayly as he led the insect orchestra. As far as we could hear through the

47

Music of the Wild

forest his musicians followed his lead unceasingly, their notes rising and falling in volume, and they even played in flight. I could not see how they flew, and fiddled on the wingshields at the same time, but repeatedly I saw them do it.

Watching above me to try to learn how this music of flight was made, I forgot the locusts and began considering the roof of the forest. The branches lapped and interlaced so closely that I felt, if I had power to walk inverted like a fly, I could cross them as a floor. There was constant music up there, and the dominant note was the crow's, while the sweetest was the wood pewee's. There were many places where in the stout branching of tall trees the crows had built a sitting-room of a bushel of coarse twigs and lined it with finer material. Now all the families had moved out and gone picnicking among the trees.

None of them evinced retiring dispositions. They appeared alike at that height, and all I could **A Crow** tell of them was that they were crows. Their mu- **Solo** sic was constant and, where undisturbed by our presence, of most interesting character. I could distinguish three distinct calls. They frequently uttered a gutteral croak that seemed to translate "All right!" Then there was a sharp, vehement "Caw! Caw! Caw!" warning those of the family farther away of the fact that there was something unusual in the forest. It was used at a time and

48

A CROW SOLO

"The crow doth sing as sweetly as the lark
When neither is attended; and I think
The nightingale, if she should sing by day,
When every goose is cackling, would be thought
No better a musician than the wren."
—*Shakespeare.*

The Chorus of the Forest

in the manner of a human being crying, "Look out!
Some one is coming!" Then there was a syllabi-
cated cry, consisting of five notes, that was their
longest utterance and was delivered with tucked
tail, half-lifted wings, and bobbing head, as if to
make the speech impressive by gesture as well as
sentiment. It scarcely would do to write of this
production as a song, perhaps it might be called a
recitative, to give it a little musical color. In very
truth it resembled plain conversation and was used
at such times and in such manner as to lead me to
believe that passing crows were remarking to their
friends: "Everything is all right with me. How
goes life with you?"

I am rather fond of crows. They are so lov-
ing to each other that they arouse sentiment in my
breast. I believe they pair for life, and both of
them defend their nests and young with reckless
bravery. Good qualities, surely! They are know-
ing birds and early learn to distinguish a hoe from
a gun. When they find you without firearms they
become impudent and inquisitive, and allow you to
approach very close. There is proof that they are
individual birds because they are used constantly
as the basis of comparison by men who call each
other "wise as a crow," "black as a crow," "as sly,"
and "as cunning."

Whether crows are all these things in freedom
would be difficult to prove, since they scarcely ever

51

nest at a height of less than thirty-five feet, and from that up to fifty. At that distance it is not possible that male and female or different pairs can be told apart without strong glasses; where there is one family there are sure to be others close, and no matter how impudent a single crow may be when you are without a gun and meet him foraging in your fields, he is a wary bird when you approach his nest.

In captivity crows have been known to do many peculiar things of their own initiative, such as hid- **"Black as** ing food given them when they are not hungry, for **a Crow"** use at another time, or rubbing against a stone a caterpillar to free it from spines. They can be taught to talk by splitting the tips of their tongues, and can repeat from two to six words distinctly and at appropriate times. In life they never are quite so black as they are painted, for the neck and back feathers have beautiful purplish bronze tints in strong light. These crows appeared to have a sense of humor, for when we left the forest without having interfered with them they seemed to imagine they had vanquished us and followed for a distance, crying something that sounded much more like, "Haw! Haw! Haw!" than "Caw!"

I never have made an exhaustive study of crows, but I have penetrated their life history somewhat, enough to get all that can be learned by seeing and hearing; and that, come to think of it,

THE WHITE CLOUD

Through the forest's darkening emerald,
In the murky, pungent gloom,
Shines a cloud of wondrous whiteness,
Where He sets the dog-wood bloom.

The Chorus of the Forest

is all I want. In my wanderings afield I often
find ornithologists killing and dissecting birds, bot-
anists uprooting and classifying flowers, and lepi-
dopterists running pins through moths yet strug-
gling; each worker blind and deaf to everything
save his own specialty, and delving in that as if
life depended, as perhaps it does, on the amount
of havoc and extermination wrought. Whenever
I come across a scientist plying his trade I am al-
ways so happy and content to be merely a nature-
lover, satisfied with what I can see, hear, and re-
cord with my cameras. Such wonders are lost by
specializing on one subject to the exclusion of all
else. No doubt it is necessary for some one to do
this work, but I am so glad it is not my calling.
Life has such varying sights and songs for the one
who goes afield with senses alive to everything. I
am positive I hear and see as much as any scientist
can on the outside of objects, for I have recorded
with my cameras a complete life history of many
birds no one else ever photographed, and to prove
it I can reproduce the pictures for the delight of
humanity. Who ever was exhilarated by seeing a
scientist measure the intestines and count the bones
of any bird? I have sent the botanical masters
flowers and vines not yet incorporated in their
books, but I was very careful to confine myself to
the least specimen that would serve their purpose.
I have hatched the eggs, raised the caterpillars,

55

Music of the Wild

wintered the cocoons, and had the rarest moth of our country emerge beside my pillow, and sent by the hundred the eggs of mated pairs to scientific men who lacked personal experience with the species. I am not missing anything, and what I get is the palpitant beauty and pulsing song of existence. The happy, care-free method is to go to the forest in early spring, and with senses alive to everything and deliberately follow the changes of the season.

One of the first sights to attract the attention will proclaim itself from afar: the flowering of the dogwood. Sometimes there is a real tree in undisturbed forest, lifting to the light a white head that makes a point of splendor. The bloom is a peculiar thing, resembling poinsettia in that the showy spathes, commonly called flowers, are merely a decoration surrounding the true bloom, which is small and insignificant. In reality what appears to be white flower petals are just wrapping that all winter has screened the little flower bud from frost and storm, and the small dent in the top of each leaf is where the very tip blighted in severe weather. After a wonderful spring exhibition the dogwood ceases to attract attention and resembles its surroundings until fall. Then its leaves begin to color early and outdo almost all others in vivid tints, added to which are the ripened berries of bright Chinese-red. Dogwood is not rare, and

The Excuse of Beauty

56

MOTHS OF **THE** MOON

'T is Nature's greatest secret, told as a priceless boon,
In the forest I heard the night moth whispering to the moon:
"Lend thy light for my courting, if thrice in thy glory I fly,
Then, from estatic loving, of joy will I gladly die."

The Chorus of the Forest

beauty is the excuse for its being, in this book at
least. Really it seems as if that might be its best
reason for appearing in the forest as well.

The big delicate moth of deep wood must enter
on the same ground, for no other among wood folk
is so quiet. The only music it could be said to make
is the chorus of delighted exclamation that greets
its every appearance before humanity; music by
proxy, as it were, for the moth is the stillest crea-
ture. The exercising imago, walled in its cocoon,
among the leaves of earth, makes more sound
than the emerged moth. There is a faint noise of
tearing as the inner case is broken and the tough
cocoon cut for emergence. Once in the air and
light, if those exquisite wings make a sound it is
too faint for mortal ears to hear.

June is the time for appreciative people to sing
in praise of the moths, but sometimes they are
double-brooded and specimens exact their share of
worship in August, as did the beautiful pair I
found clinging to a walnut tree in the forest. No
other moth is so exquisitely shaped or of such deli-
cate shades. The female is a little larger, her an-
tennæ are narrower, and her colors paler than the
male's. The white violet is not of purer white than
his body; his crisp, long-trailed wings of a bluish
pale-green, faintly edged with light yellow and set
with small transparent markings, and his legs and
feet and the heavy fore-rib of the front wings are

59

lavender. He was delicate and fragile as the bloom of a tropical orchid, and reminded me of one as he lightly hung to the rough walnut bark. They were only that day emerged, and their wings were not yet hardened sufficiently to bear their weight, so they clung wherever I placed them and posed in the most obliging manner. But the guide and I made all the music.

While I worked, over my head, all above the forest, and around the outskirts sailed the beautiful and graceful little dusky falcons. No charge **Falcon** of quietude can be made against them; they are **Music** really noisy, which can not be said of great hawks. Falcons are very handsome, and parade their beauty as if they realized it. They are by far the best-dressed members of the hawk family. The very light color of their breasts is delicately shaded, as is the bronze of their backs. Their cheek feathers are white to a narrow line above the eyes, and crossed by two parallel lines of black. They can erect a small crest, which is tinted with dull blue, and their long, graceful wing and tail feathers are tipped with white. Their beaks have the hawklike curved point for tearing. Their unusually large eyes wear a soft expression, giving to them a wise appearance. They attack small birds occasionally, but live mostly on field mice, moles, grasshoppers, and moths; so they are in evidence in the fields, and people are familiar with them. They like to watch

DUSKY FALCON

"I know a falcon swift and peerless
As e'er was cradled in the pine;
No bird had ever eye so fearless,
Or wing so strong as this of mine."
— *Lowell.*

The Chorus of the Forest

grain fields from the vantage of a telephone wire, and their graceful downward sweep when they sight prey is a beautiful thing to see.

They nest in hollow trees and bring off broods of five and six young, from their first feathering closely resembling the elders. These young are very social and make charming pets, becoming wholly domesticated in a few days. If not exactly the same, they are very similar to the falcons used by royal British women in the sport of hawking, and the small birds that we see in old prints and paintings perching on gauntlet or saddle-pommel must have been great pets with their owners. They are the musicians of the hawk and falcon families and have all their relatives talked into almost complete silence. "Ka-tic, a-tic, a-tic!" they cry as they dash after moth or grasshopper, millions of which one pair will take from a field in a season, making them a great blessing to a farmer. Full-fed and happy they swing on the ever-present telephone wire and repeatedly sing in a liquid, running measure entitled to be classed as very good music, "Tilly, tilly, tilly!"

By no stretch of imagination could the big hawks be coupled with melody. They are the kings of the treetops, but they use a sign language that all other birds readily translate. Their home in large trees is often founded on a crow's last year's nest. They use signals in courting, caress

Music of the Wild

their young tenderly, and fearlessly attack any-
thing threatening danger to them. So long as they
are unmolested and happy they are silent: a strange
reversal of the law of music in birdland. Almost
without exception other birds sing in bubbling ec-
stasy when they are happy, and mope in silence,
broken only by a few pathetic notes of wailing,
when in trouble.

The hawk gives warning when angry by a stri-
dent hiss, much like a vulture or eagle. When he
really makes an attack, for the purpose of van-
quishing an enemy, comes his one musical effort.
His battle-hymn is a hair-raising scream: shrill,
loud, and the wildest note of the forest. Small
birds flee from it in utter consternation, and no
doubt great ones quail, even if they remain to
fight. Never a hawk-scream shivers through the
treetops but a bedlam of crow-calls answer, for
they are sworn enemies. Of course the hawk by
reason of greater strength and size must win in
every battle it wages, but there is nothing to pre-
vent crows from seeing how closely they can skim
danger and raising all the excitement possible.

No bird of field or forest has the force of ex-
pression to be found on the face of a big hawk.
There is character, dignity, defiance, and savagery
combined. The eagle has a wicked, fierce appear-
ance, and I never have seen its face express any-
thing else. I can find no better terms than "dig-

64

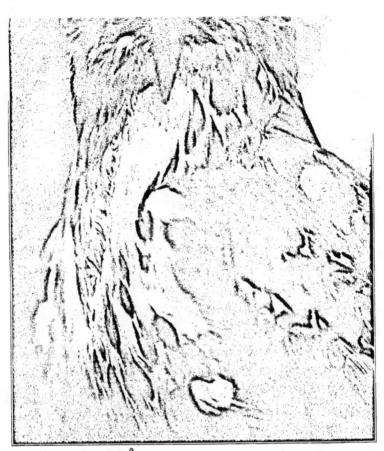

WHAT DOES HE SAY?

"I shall not ask Jean Jacques Rousseau
If birds confabulate or no.
'T is clear that they were always able
To hold discourse—at least in fable."
                    —Cowper.

The Chorus of the Forest

nity" and "defiance" to portray my conception of a hawk's facial expression, and that is not very clear. Perhaps what I am striving to convey is the idea that some things might be too cruel for the hawk; the eagle appears inexorable. If he has any mercy it is never indicated in his face. The hawk suggests to the mind that he might at least *consider* mercy. Then in poise of flight that carries him across the heavens by the hour without perceptible wing motion he is the equal of the eagle and vulture, and in keenness of vision he slightly outclasses them. Perhaps if we had been compelled to strain our eyes for generations, from his heights, in order to find our food, we would develop sight as far-reaching as his.

Serenely sailing the skies, the hawk suddenly comes darting earthward like a down-aimed arrow, in a marvelous exhibition of flight, and arises with a snake, rabbit, or bird in its claws, proving a range of vision far beyond ours. In his wonderful powers of flight and sight, in his grace and royal bearing, in the dignity of his silence, and the strength of his cry, he is one of the finest birds that live, and the most beneficial to us. For while he occasionally takes a young chicken that we intended to eat, his steady diet is snakes, moles, field mice, and grasshoppers, all of which constantly menace the land owner.

But in the evolution of nature, that seems to

Music of the Wild

provide for even minutest details, the hawk has his place and his purpose. In order that he may not become a burden when he levies upon us, he is given only two nestlings, while we raise chickens by the hundred; and the game birds upon which he preys as a rule number from fifteen to twenty in a brood, like quail, rail, and ducks. There is further to be considered that a warning of the hawk's descent is almost universal in field and forest. If the scratching hen does not see him, a nearby cock does; and if wild mothers are busy searching for food there is the bluejay to tell on him, and so the strongest of his prey take to cover and he gets only the weakling, that is best removed from the brood for the sake of the health of those remaining or of young it might raise.

There is not much to be said for hawk music, yet the voice of the forest would lose the charm **The** of its wildest note were this great bird extinct, and **Wildest** it is because it is wild and different from sounds **Note of** **the Forest** of every day that we love it. Then, as a picture seen from afar, the forest never would be complete without these birds of tireless wing hanging over it and reigning upon their thrones of air. So I hope earnest consideration will be given these points in favor of the royal bird before another of its kind is dropped from its high estate.

Up where the hawk chants his battle-hymn, the crow chuckles, and the pewee wails, outlined clearly

68

A BEECH TREE HARP

> —"*you scarce would start,*
> *If from a beech's heart*

The Chorus of the Forest

against the sky could be seen the finely-toothed
cutting and waxy gold-green leaf that only could
mean beech, and I marveled. Could beech branches
be waving there? That tree of low habit and A Beech-
Tree Harp
spreading limb! I called my guide's attention
to it, and he made a road, and then cleared space
for me to focus. Where trees were so numerous
it was impossible to get away far enough to in-
clude the entire subject. This mighty wind instru-
ment of the forest was fourteen feet in circum-
ference and fifty feet to the branching. We could
secure no leaves, but they were large and appeared
especially waxy. The trunk was the most beauti-
ful I ever have seen save the purple beeches of
Southern Indiana. Those are low, of widely-
spreading branch, and their trunks are like pur-
plish-gray moleskin. This forest beech had patches
of moleskin, then gray and green spaces, the fore-
runners of lichens, and then the lichens themselves
in big circles with exquisite gradations of gray,
white, and green colors.

At its base grew a fern with fronds two feet
long, and the mottled brown carpet spread beneath
it was deep layers of dead leaves. Then we began
to watch for its kindred through the forest, and
found many, giants all of them. One thing we
noted in particular. Not a beech ever leaned or
curved, but in a noble column all of them aspired
straight toward heaven, and among their stiff,

71

widely-spreading branches the wind sang in louder cadence than where limbs were more closely placed and of heavier leafage.

There were maples of even greater circumference and height, but many of them leaned and twisted. Their bark was not so beautiful, and their leaves not of such fine texture, but they were more artistically cut; and as these trees flourished and grew old in this damp place, the lichens had covered them almost entirely, and so they were gay with gray and green. It is peculiar how in the forest one thing seems to lead to or bear some relation to another. In examining the maples to see how far out the large branches the lichens extended, I noticed what I easily might have mistaken for a knot-hole if previous experience had not taught me to recognize the nest of the distinctive bird of the forest; a nest that is a miracle, from which come birds to match it, and they sing a song that all ornithologists agree almost breaks the heart with its sadness.

The professional "wailer" of the forest is the wood pewee; and I should like to engage him to "wail" at my funeral, I would ask no finer music. He is just a small olive-gray bird, touched with brown, his habitat high among the big crows, owls, and hawks, that comparatively must appear larger to him than an elephant does to us. Because he is evolved in God's great scheme of things to work

A Professional "Wailer"

PROFESSIONAL "WAILERS"

"Long drawn and clear its closes were— Like beggared princes of the wood,
  As if the hand of music through   In silver rags the birches stood;
The sombre robe of silence drew   The hemlocks, lordly counselors,
A thread of golden gossamer;   Were dumb; the sturdy servitors,
  So pure a flute the fairy blew.

In beechen jackets patched and gray,
  Seemed waiting spellbound all the day
That low, entrancing note to hear,—
  'Pe-wee! pe-wee! peer!'"
                                    —Trowbridge.

The Chorus of the Forest

among the treetops he is provided with wisdom and
preculiarly protected by nature. His coat is the
color of bark, his location is a lichen-covered limb,
his nest a small flat bowl of finest twigs, grass-
lined, and shaped to reproduce exactly the knots
on the trees around it, and then covered with
lichens to match those closest. This covering is
deftly bound with spider webs passing under the
limb and around the nest securely. When the
young emerge and feather. like separate seeds of
the globe of a dandelion is the down that covers
them, and in their nest or on the limb beside it,
behold! they appear as lichens too. We noticed
how inconspicuously colored the elders were, how
they matched the treetops and the nest some time
deserted, and how deft they were at twisting and
turning on wing—real acrobats,—so that no other
birds of field or forest are better protected or so
sure to bring off a brood in safety.

Then why this very mournful music recorded by
every ornithologist who ever wrote of them? The
answer is, there is no sadness in their song. In
all of a long and varied acquaintance with them I
have found them particularly jolly small birds,
safe above the average, much closer heaven than
any other of their size. They are not of doleful
disposition, and no inconsolable grief is theirs.
They are true children of the forest, and in its
solemn silences, in the slow wail of its winds, in

Music of the Wild

the sucking sobs of its rocking branches they have composed a song in harmony with their surroundings; but to our ears this music contains the notes with which we express solitude, silence, and heartbreak.

But the pewee knows nothing of this. All day True Forest Notes he sings, *and all of the season,* which proves him a particularly happy bird, not dependent upon the intoxication of the mating fever or encouraging a brooding mate with his notes. He sings as the poet, because there is an all-the-time song in his heart. In the great forest his notes fell to us slowly and serenely; why should he bubble and gurgle like a bobolink? He of the majesty and solitude of the forest! He of the high choir in the house of the Almighty! Long-drawn, clear, aching with melody, through the solemn silence of the forest, high above you comes his "Pee-a-wee," and just when you are wondering if that is all, he adds, "Peer!" It is rather a stretch of the imagination to call these notes a song; cry would seem closer, but they are the sustained utterance of the bird. His variations consist in repetition, with differcut modulation and in unequal measure.

I could detect that in the morning he hastened a little, as if the business of life were too pressing for the usual wait between notes. At noon, when all other birds were drowsy with heat and scarcely a song was heard, he broke the silence; and in the

PAPAW BLOOM

He who breathes the enchanted air,
With eyes aflame and cheeks aglow,
Knows that earth holds no spot so fair
As where the papaw lilies blow.

The Chorus of the Forest

evening, when others were singing vespers, he
stood on tiptoes, and reaching his limit for his
highest note with which to surpass them, in a posi-
tively lazy manner slid sobbingly down the scale
to his last clear utterance. At the instant we mis-
guided mortals were shuddering over the heart-
break in these wailing, long-drawn notes the little
rascal was turning somersaults in the air, darting
here and there after a fly, his sharp mandibles
clipping together when he missed until the sound
came to us on the ground far below. He was
the happiest little creature of song and dance that
wore a feathered coat.

Beside his tree grew another that made me
wonder why, since from the inception of art dec-
orators, designers, and painters have gone to the Art in
forest for copy, they did not use this. From the the Forest
frequency with which our artists work over de-
signs of fern, violet, goldenrod, and sweet brier,
one might be forgiven the supposition that with
these, material was exhausted. I think the truth
is that these good folk kept to the fence or turned
back at the gateway, and never penetrated to the
heart of the forest. Things infinitely more beau-
tiful than those that have been used are waiting
to be discovered and familiarized. Finding almost
a tree for size ladened with velvety big green fruit
made me think of studies of papaw bloom that
I had made early in the season.

Music of the Wild

Botanists and farmers may know the flower; do others? And does some one ask what it has to do with music? I am coming to that. Early in the season, when the smooth gray-green stems are pulsing with sap, when the tender yellow-green leaves are just unsheathing and not over an inch in length, the papaw lilies blow. I never heard any one else call them lilies, but I will persist in it; they are lilies, and most exquisite ones. The flowers hang lily fashion, their petals are thick, of velvety lily texture, and look at their formation! Those outside are beautifully veined and curled, of the loveliest wine-red; the inside smaller, slightly lighter in color, and set across the meeting of the outer ones, and a yellow-green pistil, pollen dusted in the heart.

I can say almost positively that Japan does not produce this tree. If she did, long ago her artists would have seized upon its magnificent possibilities for decoration. The height of simplicity so loved by them can be found in the smooth stems, the long, tender golden leaves, and the tinkling wine-colored lilies nodding in clusters over bushes so large that, where undisturbed in the forest, they attain the size of trees. Sometimes the flowers hang singly, sometimes in pairs, and most often from four to six grow in a head, so that by crowding their faces are upturned, and their full beauty displayed in wondrous fashion. They are of sweet

PAPAWS AND SUNSHINE

Leaf hidden are the frosty green papaws,
In their jackets snugly rolled,
But the sun sifts down 'til he finds them,

The Chorus of the Forest

odor, and the bees come swarming around them, with their low, bumbling, humming music, from early morning until dark. If only I were a poet, how glad I would be to transcribe for them the song that they awake in my heart!

Its name should be, "Where the Papaw Lilies Blow." I would tinge the sky with the purple of red bud, fill the air with the golden haze of tree bloom, and perfume it with the subtle odor of tree pollen. In deep shadow the earth should lie covered with a crust of late snow, and in the sun with the whiter snow of bloodroot bloom. The velvety maroon-colored lilies should distil their perfume as the wind rocked them, and among the branches the slender, graceful, bronze-backed cuckoo should prophesy April showers as he searched for food. From a nearby pool with crazy laughter a flock of loons that had paused in migration for a drink should arise from the water and plow the northward air with their sharp beaks; and an opossum should nose among the leaves for frozen persimmons. And he who breathed this enchanted air and saw these things should learn that in all nature he would find no greater treat than to linger where the papaw lilies blow. I offer this gratis to any one who has the genius to use it rightly.

With the falling of the flowers the artistic possibility of the plant only begins, for there follow large leaves of varied shadings, prominently veined

83

and finely shaped for conventionalizing, and in clusters beneath them the papaws, that must be seen to know how beautiful they are. Five and six to a cluster they hang, when young the skin a cold blue-green; with ripeness they take on a pale yellow shading, and the "bloom" of the fruit becomes like frosted velvet. The pulp is bright yellow and good to eat if you are fond of rich sweets. The seeds are large, black, and resemble those of the melon. If not gathered, the fruit hangs until winter, turns to the purple wine color of ripe Concord grapes, falls to the ground, and in the spring the seeds sprout and produce new plants.

Sometimes when taking pictures I get more than I intend. In making this study of papaw **A Ray of** leaves and fruit a ray of sunshine crept through **Sunshine** an interstice of the forest and fell across my subject. So long as the picture lasts the sunbeam lives. A lens loves bright colors and sets them on a photographic plate with peculiar brilliancy. It would be a fine thing if we could get a focus on life's sunshine and reproduce it indelibly on our hearts as stored warmth for gray days, just as the lens caught this ray of light streaming across the face of the papaw study. The truth is we do not appreciate the sunshine we have in our lives. Even more, many of us never know that we are having bright days until we are plunged into the depths of trouble and darkness; and when we grope

BANEBERRY AND MAIDENHAIR

Baneberry white and tall maidenhair,
Mingled their leaves in the perfumed air,
Teaching a lesson worthy of thought,
For the love of God was what they taught.

to find our way, and struggle to realize our condition, we suddenly learn that our sunshine is gone and life is gray monotony.

The largest open space we found underfoot was on the side of a hill or incline facing east. The trees appeared quite as large and closely set, but for some reason the earth was not covered with shrubs and bushes, as was the rule. We had found two places where trees had been cut so long ago that the decayed stumps crumbled at a touch, and there was a third not as old. Close beside it I found beauty to gladden the heart of musician, poet, or painter. It began with a white baneberry of marvelous grace. The plant was all of three and a half feet in height, a smooth stem, upright as the trees around it, and, like them, branching. Its finely cut, lacy leaves, beautifully veined and notched, grew in clusters of three. On a single stem, borne high above the leaves, shone a big bunch of china-white berries, three dozen by count; the stems red, each berry having a purple-black eye-spot. Close by grew a near relative, very similar except that its berries were red. The flowers of both are a pyramidal cluster made up of a mass of small white blooms.

Now just in front of the baneberry grew the most graceful of all ferns, the plumy maidenhair, and because of this wet season it had attained unusual size for our climate. On wiry two-foot stems

Baneberry and Maidenhair

87

Music of the Wild

waved leaves a foot and a half across. I was ac-
customed to stems of from six to nine inches in
length and leaves of eight-inch diameter. As a
finishing touch, beneath the fern, with fuzzy leaf
of peculiar shape that could not be called round
because it was wider than long, and deeply cut
where the stem joined, and with bell-shaped, ma-
roon-colored cup blooming so close the root that
I had to remove the dry leaves to earth to find the
flower, grew wild ginger. I examined this partie-
ularly because I know a writer who has the hardi-
hood to compare this grimy little burrower of the
soil with papaw bloom, that has six artistically
cut petals, each of which is of much richer color
and texture, and large enough to make a perfect
ginger flower.

In removing dry leaves around the ferns and
digging out the ginger I unearthed a music-box,
The Song of the Cricket and learned a lesson. I always had thought the
cricket a sort of domesticated insect, beginning
with "The Cricket on the Hearth" and ending
with one that sang for the greater part of last
winter in our basement. A few weeks earlier I
had learned in an oat field many miles away that
there were more big black crickets under an oat
sheaf where it lay in a low, damp place than I
ever had seen elsewhere in all my field work. Now
the forest taught me that the cricket in my cabin
was a prisoner, lost from home and friends, and

CRICKET MUSIC

"The cricket tells straight on his simple thought—
Nap, 't is the cricket's way of being still."

—Lanier.

The Chorus of the Forest

those beneath the oats scouts searching for food; the army was around decaying wood and below deep layers of leaves on the floor of the forest.

In a glittering black mass they poured out by the thousand when disturbed; some in their haste leaped upon the backs of those in front and ran over them. Of course, I know there are differing species of the cricket family that choose suitable locations. I am merely stating that the largest, most prosperous branch in the whole world lives in the forest.

When I made this study grasshoppers sang around the fence, and many strayed to the interior, so that their notes came almost constantly; but by close listening you could distinguish fractions of a second when their voices were silent. Many katy-dids homed there and boasted much of the prowess of their ancestors. Locusts answered each other in rapid succession, but you could separate the call from the answer. To the "Chirr-r-r-r-r!" of the crickets there was no beginning and never the hint of an ending. Millions of these shining, black-coated little musicians sang in concert and unceasingly. There was no question but their voices formed the dominant insect note of the forest.

Crickets are not compatible with good house-keeping because they cut fabrics. But of all in-sects people tolerate them most. One little piece

Music of the Wild

of exquisite writing has made life easier for the family. A cricket walks unharmed where a heavy The foot crushes a grasshopper or locust. The cricket Cricket on one hearth has made a welcome for all crickets, on my Hearth and the home boasting one that will sing late in the season feels that it has materialized evidence of good cheer. I know how vainglorious we were over a cabin cricket that once homed with us, how all other sound ceased when he began to sing, and how we never failed to call the attention of visitors to him, and how disappointed we were if he did not perform when we were expecting he would. A cricket makes fine, cheery music, the natural accompaniment to the snapping crackle of an open wood-fire, which is the only rational source of heat in a real home. I could write a larger book than this on fire forms, flame colors, and the different tints of smoke ascending from logs of various trees as they burn in my fireplace. If my dreams as I watch the flames materialized on my library shelves instead of ascending the chimney with the smoke, no one would produce so many fine volumes as I. The cricket is so a part of the dreams that a tone of his happy song should run through all of them.

The wings are the musical instruments, and with these crickets obtain so closely to the sound of a voice that people always speak and write of them as "singing," though they really are instru-

EBONYMUS AMERICANUS

*"This is not solitude; 't is but to hold
Converse with nature's charms, and view her stores unrolled."*

The Chorus of the Forest

mental performers, the same as the grasshopper, locust, and katy-did.

These wings are attached back of the shoulders and are so short they cover not more than the middle third of the body. They are so very small, music must be their greatest use. I do not believe they would bear the weight of the insects in flight, but by spreading and beating them they might assist in long leaps. The remainder of their anatomy is complicated. Our cabin cricket was smaller and lighter brown than its big, forest relatives, but they appeared quite similar. Their outer covering encases them as armor. Their eyes are prominent and glittering, and help to give them a cheerful, alert appearance. I noticed that when traveling undisturbed they lightly touched objects before them with their long hair-fine antennæ as if feeling their way. On each side of the front section of the bodies are a series of three short legs used for walking, and just back of these the large, long leg for leaping.

On the floor, pottering over cricket history, close to the fence, where the light was strong, I made a new acquaintance. Botanists may know it well, but I am unable to place it in any of many valuable works I own. This may be because I found it in the fall, at berry-bearing time, and they would describe it in bloom. But I have small trouble in identifying other plants at any season.

Music of the Wild

A New Ac-
quaintance No nature-lover has described this as I found it, and no decorator has conventionalized it; yet surely the berries stand close the head of the beauty class. Brilliant color of Chinese-red and coral-pink attracted me, and on investigation I found a plant of half bush, half vining habit, close two feet in height, its stems straight, round, slender, faintly bluish-green, its leaves shaped much like and resembling in veining and color those of some plum trees I know. It had seeded in a burr, shaped and toothed outside like that of a beechnut, but almost four times larger, and of warm coral-pink color. These burrs hung over the plant profusely from very long, fine threads of stems, and being ripe, had burst open, revealing four partitions covered by a thin Chinese-red membrane. In some this had opened in a straight line down the middle, drawing back each way, and evicting at the four points of the pink burr a bright-red berry fastened by an extremely short stem. These were really a seed, of pearl color, oval, and a little oblong in shape, one end touched with flecks of red like a bird's egg, and enveloped in a red, pulpy cover. I have found this plant only four times in all my life afield, and for brilliant color and complicated arrangement of seeding I do not remember its equal. *Ebonymus Americanus* is its resounding scientific name. If it is sufficiently well known to have a common one I can not find it.

A GROUND MUSICIAN

What do you think!
He tells you his name,
And it is "Che-wink."

The Chorus of the Forest

While I photographed it a rustling among the deep leaves called my attention to the typical bird of the forest floor, but this was not our first meeting; in fact, we were old acquaintances, and one box of negatives in my closet at home recorded all of its nesting history that I could secure with a camera. Studies of this bird are unusual, at least I am fairly well informed along this line, and I never have seen any published. It is typical of the forest floor. It not only builds and raises its young on earth, but finds food there, scratching like an exemplary hen, with feet working alternately, and also surpassing her by using both feet at once, in a manner she never learned. It has scratched and scratched until from much scratching its length of toe and nail has developed into its most conspicuous part. On the same principle, but in different members, the heron has evolved its long legs by wading among the reeds. Because constant flight keeps them useless, two of a kingfisher's toes are yet grown together and do not separate as do those of perching birds. You only have to notice the feet of this family group to observe the extraordinary length of toe and nail, even in the young.

I suspect you are wondering why I do not tell their name. There is no necessity. The bird prefers to introduce itself. Indeed, there is every probability you have heard it do so many times,

A Ground Musician

99

while you never have seen the vocalist, for it keeps close earth in damp, dark places, although social and a constant talker. It mounts to a high choir-loft to sing its song. The cricket's is the dominant insect note of the forest in August, the crow's the bird voice of the treetops; this is the busybody and the unceasing musician of earth.

Pairs remain together after family cares are over, and their conversation consists of a question and an answer. "Che-wink?" inquires the male, with strong interrogative inflection on the last syllable. "Che-wee!" exclaims the female, in reply, as if she were delighted to say so. "Che-wink?" he asks again, with his next breath. "Che-wee!" she gurgles, as if she were telling him something "perfectly splendid" for the first time. This call of the male supplies the species with a common name. On his part it means, "Where are you?"— and her answer is, "Here!" But as it is delivered I think, from the spontaneity of the reply, that it means a shade more—"Safely here!" "Happily here!" or "Glad to be here!"

I am sure this is true, because in work close chewink nests I have had much acquaintance with them. If a male calls and does not get instant reply, he repeats the notes with perceptibly higher tone and stronger inflection. If there is no answer to this he flies to a bush and begins a perfect clamor of alarm cries, and hurries around the

TALL BLUE BELLFLOWER.

"'Neath cloistered boughs, each floral bell that swingeth
And tolls its perfume on the passing air,
Makes Sabbath in the fields, and ever ringeth
A call to prayer."

—Smith.

The Chorus of the Forest

location, keeping up and increasing the excitement until the straying female hears him and comes home. Where many of these birds nest undisturbed their notes are more noticeable than any other feathered folk of earth.

The chewink is a finch, large as a rose-breasted grosbeak, and often mistaken for one on account of the black coat and cowl worn by both. The chewink is far the more elegant and graceful bird, while the grosbeak is the better musician. Mr. Chewink wears a black coat, with the sleeves and tail touched with white, a black headdress and broad black collar. His shirt is creamy white and his vest a bright Venetian-red. Mrs. Chewink's headdress and collar are a brownish-tan color, the back and sleeves of her suit the same color with the white touches. Her waist front is a dark creamy white, and her toilet is completed with a Zouave jacket of red, a shade darker than Mr. Chewink's vest. All her colors are richer in subdued tones and more artistic than his, for where he sharply contrasts she harmonizes exquisitely. Both birds have long tails, longer legs than others of their genus, and the feet and toes as described, from much scratching.

They are the noisiest birds of the forest floor. They desire to search the earth for tiny bugs and worms, and the fallen leaves make a deep covering everywhere. So they alight on a place that

103

they select in a manner known to themselves; at times I have seen them stand motionless, with one side of the head turned toward the ground, as robins do, and appear to listen, so that I have thought it possible that they hear insect sounds, as we may if we bring our ears close earth. When a spot is chosen they jump upon it with toes wide-spread, and sink their sharp nails deeply into the leaves; then with half-lifted wings, to aid the leg and body muscles, they spring as far forward as they can and drop their load. In this manner I have seen them at one effort clear a space as large as a breakfast plate, on which to scratch for food.

Once as I crouched, covered by a tan crava-nette exactly the color of the leaves, beside a stump **A Lost** in the forest, a male bird came within six feet of **Study** me and several times uncovered the earth by this method. In each operation he appeared to listen before he selected a spot to work upon. Once my sense of humor spoiled a fine study of his mate. She was approaching the nest to feed the young, when he attempted to lift a large layer of leaves. He must have gripped securely a fine, thread-like root that lifted for a few inches and then became taut. The shock whirled him sidewise and rolled him over. He did not know what had happened, and he appeared so astonished and cried out so indignantly that I laughed and helped increase his fright. He dashed from the thicket uttering

THE CROWN OF THE FOREST KING

"What gnarled stretch, what depth of shade, is his!
There needs no crown to mark the forest's king;

The Chorus of the Forest

alarm cries that scared his mate out of focus, so
I lost a picture.

Their habit is to build on the earth beneath the
protection of a gnarled root or fallen limb, but
once I found a nest in a tangle of bushes ten
inches above ground. The female slipped from it,
hopped away, and trailed a wing that appeared to
be broken, and squealed as if wounded. I never
saw a killdeer play " 'possum" more naturally.
Chewinks build of leaves and coarse grass, and line
with finer material. The eggs are white, touched
with brown. Aside from that tribal call from
which they take their names, they sing a sustained
song of several notes, much more promising in the
beginning than in the ending, that seems so un-
necessarily abrupt as to cause one to wish to enter
protest. The song opens with a sweet, clear whis-
tle, and then slides off without at all fulfilling the
expectation it inspired. But where many musi-
cians mount the bushes and sing, accompanied by
the endless leaf rustle of their mates, the music
forms one of the most pleasing parts of the forest
chorus. They mount still higher and sing with
more abandon quite late, for birds, in the evening;
or else their notes sound particularly well at that
time on account of the peculiarity of their vocal-
izing neighbors who are just running scales to clear
their voices for the night performance.

You never can say you really belong in the for-

Music of the Wild

est unless you have remained for so many all-night concerts that you are familiar with the parts of The Midnight Serenade all the musicians. At night only a few grasshoppers are vocalizing, the crickets never cease, and the katy-dids tune up for their star performance. Daytime feathered singers as a rule tuck their heads and go to sleep early, and the absence of the wavering accompaniment of their varied voices gives peculiar pause and tonal color to ensuing notes that are of themselves sufficiently emphatic and startling. Almost always the wind drops on summer evenings, and a great silence so deep it enwraps you as a garment and fills your soul with awe seems to creep from the very heart of the forest. When not dominated by tree and bird music, insect voices ring out shrill and high, and the whippoor-will finds truly artistic pause and setting for its remarkable vocal performance. No other bird of all ornithology lifts its voice and in such clear and distinct English enunciates what it has to say. Almost every naturalist and musician afield recording bird notes disagrees as to the utterance and inflection of some of our plainest talkers. There is no difference of opinion whatever about this bird. To every one it says too plainly to admit questioning, "Whip-poor-will!"

Near the same time the night hawk takes flight during the breeding season. After family cares are over I have seen bands of them come sweeping

BLACK HAW BLOOM

Winter snowballs are cold and hard,
They often make your fingers freeze;
Summer snowballs are soft and sweet,
And you gather them off the trees.

The Chorus of the Forest

from the forest and spread over lake and river as early as four o'clock in the afternoon. They are of tireless flight, darting here and there with mouths wide open for whatever they come across, as they take their food on wing. Especially during the breeding season the males do aerial stunts, possibly for the diversion of weary mates. They soar seventy-five or one hundred feet, spread the wings and tail widely, and drop toward earth, the wind passing between the stiff feathers causing the whistling, booming sound that earns for them the name of "night jar."

This performance does jar the night somewhat, and might the nerves also, were it wise to allow ourselves such a luxury. I prefer the term to night hawk, since the birds are not nearly so much creatures of night as they should be to merit distinct designation by the name; neither are they hawks at all, but relatives of martins and swallows. Aside from this instrumental performance on wing they utter a nice, cheerful scream that some peculiar folks insist upon disliking, but then there are people in this world who are forever raising strong objections to the vocalizing of their human neighbors. Night jars have a third performance, half vocal, half pantomimic, that is most remarkable of all. When surprised close their nests, cornered, or slightly wounded, they lie on their backs, swell their facial and throat muscles

Jarring the Night

111

to astonishing size, and hiss, with mouths wide
open. So the ever-discerning French call them
"flying toads," to commemorate the performance.

I can not change the subject after this without
saying for these birds that they are beautiful, in
rich colors of blended black, gray, creamy white,
several shades of brown, and the red that scientists
designate "rufous;" combinations that render them
especial colorative protection among the grasses,
leaves, and on the earth or rocks upon which they
nest. In monetary value they are almost priceless.
They do not destroy anything of use to man, while
they gather millions of grasshoppers that are cut-
ting crops, and sift the air tirelessly for insect
pests. On wing the white bands of the quills form
a half-moon that distinguishes them from the whip-
poor-will, for which they are often mistaken.

When night envelopes the forest there travel
its dusky aisles and dark mazes three creatures of
Silent soundless wing: great, exquisitely colored night
Wings moths, owls, and bats. The moths are mostly con-
fined to the months of May and June. Few peo-
ple see and none ever hear them. Matured in a
cocoon spun by a big caterpillar, performing all
the functions of their lives under cover of the dark-
ness of night, and spending their few days in the
darkest places possible, never moving in the light
except when disturbed, one would imagine they
would be dark-gray, brown, and black in coloring.

112

BLACK HAWS

*As odd a thing as you ever saw
Is the changing color of the black haw.
All its berries hang china white;
Jack Frost paints them black some October night;
When the sun sees this ebon hue,
He veils it in 'bloom' of silvery blue.*

The Chorus of the Forest

I think most of the tints of the rainbow are represented among them. Some are palest blue-green, decorated with straw color and lavender; others are cowslip-yellow, with touches of maroon; some are tan, with pink markings, and others terra cotta, with canary-colored spots and gray lines. Some are gray, with terra cotta half-moons; others are wine-red, with tan; all are of beautiful basic color, speckled, dotted, lined, striped, and spotted with bright harmonizing or contrasting designs on their wings of softest velvet down. Some have transparent ovals so clear that fine print can be read through them, set in their wings, and most moths are large as the average warbler. They sweep so close that your face is sensitive to the disturbance of air in their passing, but you hear no sound. Their flight is soft and perfectly noiseless.

The owl can afford to be of silent wing, it so dominates the night with its voice. It would give me great satisfaction if I had some way of knowing surely whether other birds sleep serenely during its vehement serenade either to the moon or to a coveted mate, or whether they are awake and shuddering with fear.

I know how the heart of a frightened bird leaps and throbs in its small breast, and I would be glad to learn that they sleep soundly, but I doubt it. They are awake and fluttering through the darkness at such slight disturbance of other nature.

Music of the Wild

There is no difficulty whatever in learning the status of owl music among people. Repulsion and shuddering greet it everywhere. I have been making an especial study of this, and I think I have learned how it began.

The Bible contains our first authentic bird history, but ornithologists before that time in other lands, and all of them everywhere since, are unanimous in doing all in their power to discredit the vocal performance of the owl. I can not find a single reference to it in the Bible not expressly written for the purpose of inspiring fear and repulsion. Isaiah says in predicting the fall of Babylon, "And their houses shall be full of doleful creatures, and owls shall dwell there, and satyrs shall dance there."

Micah said he would "make a wailing like the dragons and a mourning as the owls." When David fell into trouble he became "like a pelican of the wilderness and an owl of the desert." Such quotations constitute the entire Bible record of the bird, and taking their cue from these,—ornithologists, nature writers, and even poets perpetuate such ideas. Proctor distinguished himself by a lengthy owl poem, from which I quote,—

> In the hollow tree, in the old gray tower,
>   The *spectral* owl doth dwell;
> *Dull, hated, despised,* in the sunshine hour,
>   But at dusk he's abroad and well:

116

THE TREES

They cut them for cabins, stables and fences,
For mauls, rakes, scoops and ladles,
They cut them for pumps, beehives and troughs,
They even cut them for cradles.

The Chorus of the Forest

And the owl hath a bride who is fond and bold,
    And she loveth the wood's deep gloom,
And, with eyes like the shine of a moonstone cold,
    She awaiteth her *ghastly* groom."

The sentiment belongs to the poet, the italics are mine. Now, would you not think that the bride who is "fond and bold," and who "loveth" her home, might have just one line of whole-souled appreciation out of a lengthy poem? But she did not get it because the people who have written the volumes compiled owl history would make have forgotten to give one minute of consideration to the viewpoint of the bird. Do you suppose that to the owl her mate is "dull, hated, despised, spectral, ghastly," and only fit company for "doleful creatures, satyrs, and dragons?" If you ever had seen her nestle close to him, rub her head against him, stroke his feathers with her beak, and heard her jabber her love-story to him, you would change your mind speedily, if that is what you have been thinking.

There is good excuse for other birds fearing the owl. It seems to be ordained by nature that the larger species prey upon the smaller for food, and they suffer from the law without being able to argue its justice. But people have nothing to fear and everything to enlist their sympathy. I think the truth is the shudder that greets the vocalizing of the owl is not really for the bird at all,

119

Music of the Wild

but a touch of fear of the forest at night, yet in the system. A taint of an inheritance from days when our ancestors battled there for existence, that becomes manifest at unexpected sounds, the gleaming surfaces of pools, the wavering shafts of moonlight, the vibrant tree-rustle of the wind, the stealthy step of animals crossing the leafy floor, the gutteral scream of night-hunters fighting over prey. So because this bird of silent wing comes hooting from a place of which they stand a little in awe they vent their displeasure on its voice.

Of all the scientists, ornithologists, and nature writers whose work graces my library shelves not **The Owls'** one goes on record with the fact that the owl ut- **Serenade** terance most loudly condemned is his *love song,* used in courting his mate, and when these writers shudder they do not explain that Mr. Horned Owl is throwing in especially intoned and emphatic sentiment. He is imploring with all his might for the mate he covets to pair with him and record a title to the first location he finds suitable for their happy home. Just singing out his heart in the best and only serenade he knows.

Because they are of night and silent flight, no doubt, bats are placed in the same class with owls— at the very foot. Most fastidious people imagine that they draw the line at a worm, but they do not. They draw it at a bat, and this, again, on account of the prejudicial history surrounding a

Fireflies flitting all around
Wouldn't stop to be eaten;
Hungry babies too young to fly,
Could such luck be beaten?

YOUNG BATS

The Chorus of the Forest

wonderful little creature, half bird, half beast.
The poet Street wrote of it as "a wavering, sound-
less blot." A bat in the face is considered just
and sufficient cause for convulsions, yet the worst
that possibly could result from it would be a tiny
scratch of a bite, not nearly so annoying as that
of a mosquito.

Once I had a face-to-face acquaintance with a
mother bat whose body bore the weight of three
young that nursed at her breast and clung to her
while they slept. She had a very small face,
shaped like that of a young pig, except that the
ears were round instead of pointed. The male
must have carried food, or else enough insects to
sustain life flew her way, for she could not carry
her burden on wing. With the exception of flight,
I could not discover one attribute or characteristic
of the feathered tribe. Her wings were not in
the least birdlike. They resembled the half of a
spread umbrella having a thin rubber cover. Each
wing represented four ribs and three sections of
cover, and these ribs centered in a joint like the
long, bony fingers of a hand, with a little sharp
hook of a thumb, by which the bat clung and
helped bear her weight. She slept head down and
was liveliest at night. Her fur was silken soft
and fine, and of beautiful red-brown color. When
fed milk with a small wooden paddle I could see
her fine sharp teeth, but she did not offer to bite.

Music of the Wild

When I had studied her all I desired and photographed the family, she was replaced where she had been found.

She appealed to me as a happy mother busy with affairs of momentous importance, for she was raising triplets instead of the usual twins of bat-land. A human touch that struck straight to my heart often occurred when the young finished nursing and crept over her body. They dug into her skin until she squealed such a sibilant, faint sound that it would have required multiplication by a million to raise one healthy note in the great chorus of the forest. I was reminded of a mother crying out when her baby hurts her. It would be well for every one to become sufficiently familiar with bats to handle them, and find out what they are doing, and why, and what their relation is to us.

Having learned these things, people will become more in harmony with the scheme of creation. They will respect the motherhood of this small winged animal, and recognize that in sifting the night air for noxious insects, as do swallows and martins by day, it is fulfilling a purpose in the plan of creation and being of inestimable value to us. If the pests exterminated by the flycatchers, swallows, martins, night hawks, and bats were allowed to multiply one season without being molested, humanity then would be ready to raise a

WHERE THE WOODS BEGIN

"To loiter down lone alleys of delight,
And hear the beating of the hearts of trees,
And think the thoughts that lilies speak in white
By greenwood pools and pleasant passages."
—*Lanier.*

The Chorus of the Forest

great chorus of praise concerning the work of these small creatures of silent wing.

If I had a lifetime to live in the forest, inexhaustible plates, indestructible cameras, wells of ink, and pens of magic, I am sure that for each day—yes, every hour—I could find some interesting thing to picture and describe. But the demands of life will not allow this, and the forest ends all too soon in these days. You can locate the line where mere woods begin by robin talk.

Here you find despoiled forest. It is easy to work, because in taking out valuable trees for commerce men have cut roads that can be followed even in quite wild places. Often many trees have been felled, and the strong light shining in has started grasses growing. Men see in these open places tender, luxuriant pasture for stock, so when salable timber is taken out the next step is to kill all the shrubs and vines possible, burn the brush, and make grazing grounds. Of course the cleared fields come next, and as they march with inexorable force, they push back the woods farther and yet farther.

I find that most of the trees are of little or no commercial value. They remain because they are of twisted growth, bent, soft wood, hollow, nut bearers, or too small to be felled with profit. So the woods belong to pasturing stock, birds, animals, and children. The lure of the unknown in

Where The Woods Begin

127

Music of the Wild

the forest is not over the open wood, but it has great attractions of its own. To most people who fancy they are "roughing it" the woods are eminently satisfactory, and as far as they care to penetrate.

In the woods you are sure to be close a road, and you know there are almost constant passers-by, in case anything annoys you. You can see your way far ahead, and walk on solid foothold, padded with thickly growing grass like a lawn. You can lie safely on a green couch with a tree for a back rest. For atmosphere you find a hint of forest pungency and coolness without the damp, mucky odor.

The music of the woods is very different from the forest. The insects are much the same, but **The Chorus of the Woods** widely scattered, so that their songs lack volume. Its birds are not of the same voice and habit, and it homes other animals. Tree music is entirely different. The density of the forest dissipates the force of even heavy wind, and the intricacy of the branches divides it into wailing, sobbing murmurs of sound. In the woods the winds can blow with might, and meet much less obstruction, so that the harp music is higher of tone, grander in sweep, longer in measure, with more of an instrumental swell.

Nut trees are spared almost universally in clearing, so they are numerous and easy to find,

128

FROST FLOWERS

The latest snow
The Spring woods know,
Is when the dainty wild flowers blow.

The Chorus of the Forest

and chattering squirrels are plentiful around them.
Hollow trees have no monetary value; they remain
and furnish shelter for everything desiring either
an upright or a prostrate home. I noticed in the
woods that dead trees had sufficient space to lie
down and decay at ease. The squirrels bark and
race along the logs, coons sniff and shuffle in them,
and the cotton-tails bound with a quick flash of
white from covert to covert. The jays are kept
busy guarding the woods. Orioles trail their bub-
bling song along their chosen paths of air. Flam-
ing cardinals chip among the bushes, and barn
owls enliven the night.

At no time are the woods ever so the property
of any human being as in early spring they belong
to the children. For the small people, it seems to Frost
me, the flowers and birds are an especial inherit- Flowers
ance from the Father. The Lord knew when He
blanketed the earth with snowy white how children
would walk long distances and overturn the dead
leaves in their search for spring flowers, because
of all others they love these most,—just the white
anemones, pink-flushed spring beauties, blue vio-
lets, and Dutchman's breeches.

No bird note I ever have heard was quite so
sweet as the voices of the children out for a first
flower-hunt after the confinement of a long, cold
winter. Without knowing what it is they love,
they lift their heads, fill their lungs with the air

131

Music of the Wild

cool with scarce melted snows, pungent with cat-
kin pollen, tinged with the vague, subtle perfume
from unsheathing leaves, and the bloom of forest
trees, and answer to the call of nature. They
hasten to the woods as cattle dry-fed for months
race through pasture when first released, too crazed
with joy to begin grazing at once. If the truth
were told, I think this love of children for the
spring flowers is almost as much craving for the
intoxication of spring air and release from win-
ter's bondage as it is appreciation of the blooms.

What a shout the child sends up who finds the
first flower! The one who secures a dogtooth vio-
let is envied as men covet each other's gold. What
matters it that the hot, close-grasping little hands
will wither the delicate frost blooms hopelessly be-
fore they can be presented so lovingly to mother
and teacher? The children have had the joy of
their outing, the fulfillment of their search, the
pleasure of giving the precious gift; and where
the earth lies blanketed with flowers until one must
look closely to see that it is not yet snow-covered,
what they take never will be missed, and the com-
ing spring will bring as profuse bloom as the past.

Later in the season, when the cardinal flower,
foxfire, cowslip, bellflower, bluebell, and daisy
bloom—flowers that are of rarer occurrence and
that would be exterminated by such vigorous at-
tacks—the children have become accustomed to

132

SYCAMORE

"In the outskirts of the village,
On the river's winding shores,
Stand the Occidental plane-trees,
Stand the ancient sycamores."
  —*Whittier.*

The Chorus of the Forest

freedom and out-door sports, and seldom go to the woods.

I once knew an Irishman who, in reference to being greedy about anything, said it was always his way to "take a little and leave a little." I wish I could impress this splendid doctrine upon all flower hunters, especially city folk who go pleasure-driving through the country. Frequently while at my work in the fields and woods I meet them, and they never leave anything, not even the roots, unless it be wild rose, goldenrod, or something so profuse they can not possibly take all. That is not the worst. They are not prepared to gather flowers. They see a lovely red, blue, or yellow bloom, and jump from their carriages long enough to drag up the plant by the roots. If the flower is a hardy annual, this means death. If a seedling, it is death also, for no seed remains to ripen. I hope that I may live to see the day when our wild flowers will be protected by law, the same as our birds.

If the flowers had been created to furnish sweets for honey-gatherers and feeders only, all of them might as well have been green or have consisted merely of stamen and pistil. I never will believe that the gorgeously colored petals are only a signal to attract bees and butterflies. The theory is confounded in the beginning by the differing colors and the fact that many brilliant flow-

"Take a Little and Leave a Little"

135

ers have no perfume whatever and are not visited by sweet-lovers. If color were only a signal to insects, it might as well be all red or yellow. If petals were solely an attraction to honey-gatherers, why call bees and butterflies to bloom having no sweetness? It is as sure as can be that flowers are not only for sweet-lovers, but for us, to give pleasure, to glorify the landscape, to set a joy-song singing in the soul.

Flower forms are complicated, beautiful past describing, and their colors varied to suit every degree of taste and circumstance of usage. The Lord gave the blossoms decorating the earth, as a masterstroke, a finishing touch, the patent-right of Divinity stamped upon the face of His work. Then surely it is an offense to Him ruthlessly to tear up plants by the root, and to kill them for the moment's gratification. Any one who wishes to preserve a proper spirit of gratitude to God for His gift of the flowers will cut a *few* carefully, and leave the plant to bloom another year, or mature its seed. I think, further, that any person of refined taste not only will leave a plant alive, and a part of its bloom to mature seed; but he also will leave some of its *flowers* for the next traveler of the road. The highway stretches endlessly, and human souls more sensitive than you would dream are upon it each hour. There is not always a song on every lip. The lines on some faces indicate wea-

The Patent-Right of Divinity

THE APPLES OF MAY

The mandrake stoutly raises
Its silken umbrellas green,
To shelter pearl-white flowers,
Apples of gold to screen.

The Chorus of the Forest

riness, care, and deep sorrow. Flowers and bird songs are to cheer the way for all, and some need encouragement so sorely. Possibly the very next comer may be sad-hearted, and the bright blooms would offer cheer. Who are you, to monopolize any gift of the Lord merely because you happen to be the first to find it?

The only way to make any diminution of the small spring flowers would be to plow and till the soil. But of the larger, later growths mentioned some are at present almost extinct. Ten years ago tall, blue bellflower waved in almost every fence-corner of my immediate territory. This summer vigorous search for just enough to fill an eight by ten photographic plate revealed it in only three places, widely separated. Another hunt disclosed foxfire in one location, and no cardinal flower.

In the woods where mandrake formerly grew in half-acre patches, trampling cattle and rooting pigs, aided by ruthless flower-gatherers, have Apples played havoc with it until search is required to find of May a healthy, typical growth. Mandrake is a wonderfully peculiar plant and, aside from its medicinal value, is beautiful and bears fruit. In early spring the tender leaves, wrapped around their stems like a folded umbrella, come pushing through the earth. The plants have one stalk, that branches at the height of ten or twelve inches, each branch supporting a big leaf made up of four or six sections,

139

lobed to the base, so that they appear to be separated. The flower opens at the branching, a waxy, white cup that resembles a lily in texture and has six petals. Pollen-laden stamens surround the pistil, that is straight and heavy, and on the dropping of the leaves it develops the fruit. The flowers are oppressively fragrant, but many people admire them and are fond of the ripe apples. Country children gather them just at the turning to gold, and bury them in the bran barrel for a treat long after the woods are bare. They are called "May-apples," and are entitled to be classed as the typical flower and fruit of the woods. Like many other species, extinction threatens them.

Last season from early spring I had been watching a large bed of mandrake that I hoped would bloom profusely and give me a good study for this book. Passing the location one Sabbath afternoon, I planned to stop and learn if it would be ready for use on the morrow. From afar my hopes sank, for I could see a carriage standing at the place. When I arrived one man was holding the horse, and another with two women were coming from the woods. Each one of them carried as many mandrake stems as they possibly could grasp; every stem had an exquisite waxy flower at the top, shorn of all vestige of leaf. The bed was ruined, and the ground covered with roots and leaves. If those people had not torn up, they

SMOKE HOUSE

Through cycles the sycamore lifted its head,
Above savage and beast with stealthy feet,

The Chorus of the Forest

had trampled down every plant; and the great bunches of bloom they carried would not live to reach the city, for mandrake is extremely delicate when gathered. You could have trailed the party from the woods by a milky way of petals already fallen, and no doubt the mass of flowers was discarded before ten miles had been traveled, so sensitive are these blooms to touch.

It has been my fortune to find mandrake flourishing beneath or near oak trees so often that I have wondered if there could be an affinity. From the nature of the plant, I suppose not; but this I know: foxglove loves to twine its roots around those of oaks, and finer specimens flourish near them than anywhere else. And I have been told that more delicious truffles grow among oak roots than chestnut. The oak is a wonderful tree. It reaches unrecorded age, and is strong and hardy. It becomes such a giant that it is king of the forest, unsurpassed in the woods, and has no peer in the fields. The mellow bass notes of nature's tree music are played among its massive branches. There are many varieties that are used for furniture and wherever stout, unyielding timbers are required in a house or for ship-building. In commerce it is valuable for making furniture and musical instruments, and for certain purposes no other tree will take its place.

Oak bark is very rough and deeply grooved

143

with the cracks of growth, and where the tree is
not crowded its shape is symmetrical, and its leaves
are artistically cut. In the fall some species color
with great brilliancy, crowning the king with flam-
ing red. Its flowers are long, greenish-yellow tas-
sels, pollen-covered, and their perfume is a part
of that creeping, subtle odor that people struggle
to define and can not, because they do not dream
what produces it. I always find the bees, wild and
domesticated, extremely busy over it, and so far
as I can judge by my taste it is one of the kinds
of pollen that tempers the sickening sweetness of
pure flower honey so that it is edible.

There are many attractive spring odors, but
there is difficulty in tracing some of them to their
The origin. Because they are fond of gathering cat-
Bloom- kins every one knows that willows bloom and has
ing of the
Trees become familiar with the pollen. But they do not
realize that in early spring forest, wood, and field
trees are all covered with tiny flowers heavily la-
dened with pollen, so that to the wind harping in
the branches is added the music of millions of
honey-gathering bees. Buckeye, walnut, hickory,
hazel, chestnut, ash, elm, beech, oak, in fact every
tree that bears nut, berry or seed is weighted with
masses of small bloom.

Oak flowers are not at all gaudy. They make
no display worth mentioning in comparison with
the fall coloring of the foliage. But the bursting

144

THE DESERTED CABIN

The hands that tended the cabin are still,
Toads hop over the sagging floor,
The cricket complains on the fireless hearth,
And weeds wave across the door,
But on blossom whitened old apple boughs
The birds sing gayly as of yore.

The Chorus of the Forest

of white oak-leaf buds covers a tree with a pale, silvery pinkish effect that is lovely and very showy; much more attractive than the flowers. All varieties of acorns are interesting with their shiny hulls, pointed tips, and flat bases that fit into their rough cups securely, until the nuts drop, or else at maturity are shaken out by the wind. Few of the cups fall until pushed off by the growth of the following spring. These little cups, clinging to a tree all winter, make it appear as if it might be a table spread for a fairies' tea party. The leaves of oak, and also beech, hang with the same tenacity, and in winter days of hoar-frost or drifting snow they form the most beautiful fringy and mossy sprays among the branches.

There are two peculiarities about the oak that as yet science has failed to explain satisfactorily: why it is that all through the forest, field, and woods these big trees so frequently die in the very top branches—a death that too often spreads to the roots; and why they are more frequently struck by lightning than any other tree. Government reports tell us they are, but they neglect to state the reason.

These and other large trees of the forest sometimes deceive the lumbermen who fell them by being a mere shell, and so they are left where they are cut. But nothing is ever useless, and birds and animals are quick to take possession of anything

147

Music of the Wild

men leave for them. Felled hollow trees are splendid homes for the big black chickens of the woods —the vultures. These birds find such trees very suitable, for in them are combined location, shelter, and building material. The deep inner coating of decayed wood jars loose with the fall of the tree, and the homing bird only has to turn on the point of her breast a few times in it to make a hollow, and she is ready for housekeeping. She lays a pair of delicate pale-blue lusterless eggs, much the color of a cuckoo's, but heavily mottled, and splashed with dark chocolate. In these circumstances the nest is very beautiful. The decayed wood runs the whole color scheme, from almost white through every shade of yellow, and then begins on tans and exhausts them, and then the browns. The big, speckled blue eggs are shaped like a hen's, but large as a turkey's.

The young are out in a month, and are simply comical little creatures, having the sharp, hooked beak of the flesh-eater, a little old wrinkled face of leathery appearance, and a body that expands to three times its shell capacity on the first day of emergence. Their dress is of snowy white, fine as swan's down. They are so clumsy and helpless they must remain many weeks developing in the log before taking wing and sailing to the clouds.

The old birds are relatives of Pharaoh's chickens of ancient Egypt, where they were so bene-

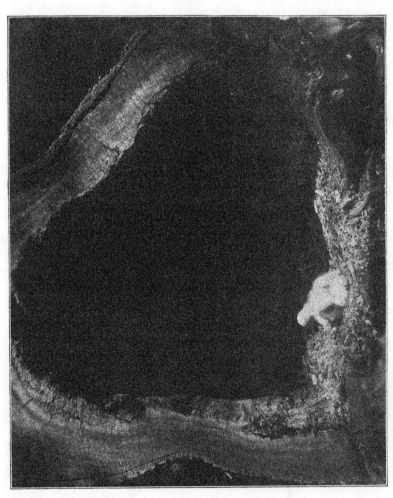

PHARAOH'S CHICKENS

"V was a vagabond vulture
Who said: 'I don't want to insult yer,
But when you intrude
Where in lone solitude
I'm a-preyin' you're no man o' culture!'"
—Riley.

The Chorus of the Forest

ficial in their work of ridding camps, tenting families, villages, and cities of refuse and decaying matter, that in the heat bred plague and fever quickly, that one of the kings surpassed the stringent laws of his predecessors for the protection of the birds by enacting a law inflicting the death penalty on any one killing a vulture. Following this precedent, some of our Southern States impose a heavy fine as a means of protecting these birds.

All over the South they are common, and at times become familiar and perch upon housetops and buildings, so contaminating the water supply that it is a question as to whether they are a blessing. In the North the birds are not numerous, but every year makes them more so. Their cousin, turkey-buzzard, is frequent. The old birds spend much of their time on wing, ranging the sky over miles of country searching for food. They are graceful and majestic in flight as any bird, not truly black, but shading from a reddish tinge to a rich dark-brown with blackish effects.

I can not see that any bird presents a more attractive picture in the sky. It is not known how high they can soar; beyond our range of vision, that is sure. Their music resembles a guttural jabber in love-making, most of which is done in sign language; and when angry or afraid, they hiss much like geese. In danger or anger they do

Black Vulture Music

151

not scream and fight with beak and feet, as the hawk or eagle, but content themselves with hissing and biting if cornered. They duck their heads, dodge rapidly, and are very dexterous in making their escape. While they appear anxious, they are not bold and will not attack you if you touch their young. Possibly this is because they consider a habit of theirs to be the best means of defense, and expect the young to protect themselves in the same manner. Their method of warfare is quite as unique and effective as that of the skunk. The staple food of these birds is carrion, and when angry or disturbed they present you with their partially digested dinners. The question whether birds have much sense of smell—above all, whether a vulture can smell itself—long has been discussed among scientists. No bird or animal is offensive to itself, but vultures must have some hazy knowledge that this act on their part is disgusting to mortals; else, why the inclination, even in the newly-hatched young? A great amount of flight and patient searching is required to secure a vulture's chosen food; surely they would not be so ready to part with it if they did not know the act would secure for them the immunity it usually does.

Vultures remain in the woods and fields until late in the fall, probably because their young need much practice before they have the strength and agility of wing for migration. Usually the leaves

HOP TREE MUSIC

Gayest music the hop trees are making,
Deep in the heart of fairyland,
To the castanets they are shaking,
Dance the pixie, gnome and fairy band.

The Chorus of the Forest

have colored, and most of them fallen, before these birds migrate. They remain with us, as the larks, until frost and cold drive them away. After the young become self-supporting the family perches among the branches of a big tree for the night. This is cold, unattractive business by November, for there is little shelter on any tree save among the dry leaves of oaks and beeches.

There is a smaller tree that once deceived me into the belief that it was clinging to its dead leaves as do its larger fellows, but examination proved that it was loaded with dry seed clusters. It was a hop tree, and the seeds were very similar to those of the slippery elm. They are almost round in shape, flat, a small oval seed in the center, a thin dry rim around it, and a twig bears from forty to sixty in one cluster. Each seed hangs from a tough, slender stem. When the wind blows the hop tree is the greatest musician of the woods. But there is no sobbing, no wailing, no sadness in its notes. It plays a happy, clipping dance tune. From every side the wind catches the flat seed surfaces and sets them shaking with an enlivening rustle, and when millions of them strike together, all the pixies, gnomes, and fairies come trooping to the hall of the woods and begin wildly dancing as the hop tree shakes its castanets.

Before you know it you come to the end of the woods. When we stop to think, the earth as

155

originally given to us was almost solid forest. Barring the oceans, a few places of desertness, the mountains and swamps, deep forest covered the greater portion of the remaining surface at the advent of man. A few feet of digging will uncover the roots of extinct forests where some of our desert land now lies.

What the character of the chorus of the forest must have been in those days one can not imagine. The notes of our great tree harps were the first sacrificed. Before the advance of civilization the trees must fall to build homes, for fires, to clear space for cultivation, and to provide furniture and implements. As the trees vanished not only their music ceased, but the songs of all the inhabitants of their branches and the residents of the earth beneath them. The voice of the forest was hushed.

So completely were the trees wiped out that not even decayed specimens, the big bass-drums, were left for the birds. Men saw many places where they could use a hollow tree, and save much time and expense. So the pump and the watering-trough were made of them. Also the bee-hive, smoke-house, ash hopper, hen's nest, sugar-water trough, feeding-troughs of all sizes, the dog kennel, bread tray, and first and most important of all should have been mentioned the cradle. Hollow trees were used in ditches where we now place

NIGHT MUSIC ON A FOREST RIVER

"Beautiful was the night. Behind the black wall of the forest,
Tipping its summit with silver arose the moon. On the river
Fell here and there through the branches a tremulous gleam of the moonlight,
Like the sweet thoughts of love on a darkened and devious spirit."
—*Longfellow.*

The Chorus of the Forest

tile, and for many other purposes, some of them very amusing. Wherever man takes possession of the gift of the Lord the forest and its music disappear.

To be sure, new music springs up in the fields to take its place, but the substitute is very mild. On account of its wild, weird, appealing strain, found nowhere else in nature, the chorus of the forest thrills the heart. It is the only place on earth where tree music can be had in perfection, and no other is like it. Great organs have been built and numerous wind and string instruments made, all in an effort to reproduce the sigh and the sob, the wail and the roar of the forest, but they forever fall short of its grandeur and majesty.

This incomparable tree harping can not be reproduced out of its element; it may be copied in parts so accurately that its tones can be recognized, but the real music of nature is when the waves of wind sweep among the boughs of trees. It is when crickets of the forest floor sing cheerily, when grasshoppers energetically play their fiddles, and locusts sow their notes on summer air. The leaf-rustle of the chewink on earth, the mournful wail of the pewee in the treetops, the impudent chuckle of the crow, and the battle-cry of the hawk, are parts of it. The scream of the night jar, the command of the whip-poor-will, and the serenade of the courting owl combine their notes.

159

Music of the Wild

It is in the bleating of the fawn, the howl of the wolf, and the gutteral growl of the bear. Every voice of each living creature lifted in joy, curiosity, pain, or anger, with the leaf-rustle or cyclonic agony of the trees, the murmur of waters, the whisper of winds, and the song of humanity plays a part. All these unite to form one great and throbbing anthem, and if you once learn this wildest of music it will become so sacred to you that its call will be with you always, and when it is most insistent you will find peace only in the forest.

PART II

Songs of the Fields

"While round your bed, o'er fern and blade,
Insects in green and gold arrayed,
The sun's gay tribes have lightly strayed;
And sweeter sounds their humming wings
Than the proud minstrel's echoing strings."
                                        —*Howitt.*

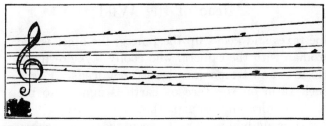

SWALLOWS

Songs of the Fields

IF the forest is the Temple of God, the fields are the amphitheater of man. When spring arouses a sleeping earth they are painted in **Field** one great, ever-shifting panorama that stretches **Music** beyond our vision, and the world is filled with the songs of nature. Because we love this music above all other we rejoice that a few old-fashioned fields remain to be flooded with such melody in its proper environment. Here, dotted with wild trees and outlined with lichen and vine-covered old snake-fences, every corner of which is filled with shrubs and bushes sheltering singing birds and insects, the great song festival of the fields is held. Here the old-time content with life is voiced from cabin homes, and the forest towering high above affords shelter and protection, and balances the forces of nature. These old farms, forest-guarded, walled by growth and moisture, resounding with bird-song and trampled with scudding feet,—all of these have two owners. One is the man who pays

165

the taxes and keeps up the fences; the other is the woman with the camera, who coolly lays down enclosures and trespasses where fancy leads. Every such farm on the face of earth is mine, also the birds, moths, and animals that it attracts.

It is undying glory to own these old cabins, the orchards that surround them, the gardens, stable lots, wood-yards, truck patches, grain fields, pastures, creeks, ponds, little hints that remind you of real forest, stretches of river, thickets, and all the insects, bird, and animal life. These farmers do not know there is another claimant to their land. They think the title is clear. No one has taught them, innocent souls as they are, that they are monopolizing all the beauty to be found in the landscape, and that beauty "lies in the eye of the beholder," and therefore it is the property of all who see and claim it for their own.

My old fields lay stretched in warm spring sunshine, mellowing slowly; for in the shelter of
Old- the forest they have not frozen and thawed repeat-
fashioned edly, as when unprotected, so the wheat crop is
Fields sure. Among last year's stubble great velvety mulleins stretch soft green leaves, and thistles prove how hardy they are. The pasture shows living green all over, and as soon as it is firm enough to bear the weight of stock the cattle that bellow disconsolately in the barnyard on dry feed will race to it like mad things.

166

DANDELION

"Dear common flower, that grow'st beside the way,
  Fringing the dusty road with harmless gold,
First pledge of blithesome May,
Which children pluck, and, full of pride uphold,
High-hearted buccaneers, o'erjoyed that they

An Eldorado in the grass have found
  Which not the rich earth's ample round
May match in wealth, thou art more dear to me
Than all the prouder summer-blooms may be."
              —Lowell.

Songs of the Fields

Northward bound wild geese dot the river bank with excrement as they pause for a short rest in their migration. The bees rim the water-trough and drink greedily, the guineas clatter, the old Shanghai rooster thrashes all his male progeny into submission, and the turkey cock wears off the tips of his wings with much strutting. The breath of earth, ice-tinged, rises to commingle with the breath of heaven, pollen-laden, and all nature becomes intoxicated with the combination. Later the sun drives the ice chill from the air, and bloomtime comes, with almost cloying sweetness.

Of the ground flowers perhaps the sweet william is most fragrant, the locust of trees, and the wild crab among shrubs, so they attract the musicians and are the best choir-lofts. Not only is the wild crab of such delightful odor that it long has been grown for the perfume of commerce, but it is more beautiful of flower than wild plum, cherry, or any of the haws. Its blossoms are not closely grouped, but hang from long, graceful stems, a few in a cluster. They have more color than any white tree bloom, being a strong red up to the day of opening. The unfolded flowers are a delicate salmon-pink inside, and retain the red on the outside. Their perfume calls wild and domesticated bees, bumblebees, wasps, and hornets, sweat bees, and every insect that ever paused at pollen and honey for a treat.

169

Music of the Wild

Much has been written about field flowers, and many poets and nature-lovers have celebrated their favorites. I sing for dandelions. If we had to import them and they cost us five dollars a plant, all of us would grow them in pots. Because they are the most universal flower of field and wood, few people pause to see how lovely they are. In the first place, the plant is altogether useful. The root is a fine blood-purifier. To a less extent the leaves partake of the same property, and they are beautiful; long and slender, reminding some scientist of the ragged.teeth of a lion—"dent de leon" —dandelion. They are of dark green color when full-grown, pale yellow-green at half growth, and if at all sheltered, almost white when young. Properly cooked, there is nothing better to eat. The bloom is a flat, round, thickly-petaled head of gold, dusted with pollen that the bees gather, and it gives a delicious tang to honey.

After a few days of bloom the flowers draw into tightly-closed heads, and stand maturing the seed. At the same time the stems *rapidly lengthen,* to lift the heads high where the wind can have free play upon them. Then at a touch, always when we are not looking, the heads open into perfect balls of misty white. These stand like crystal globes for a short time, ripening, and then the wind harvests the seed and sows it broadcast, so that the dandelion is the most universal flower that

170

ONE OF MY FARMS

"There comes a perfume from the sunset land,
And from the sunset vapor comes a voice;
Some one in evening's gateway seems to stand,
And o'er a flood of glory shout, 'Rejoice!'"
—Thompson.

Songs of the Fields

grows and the most democratic. Watch the wonderful provision of nature in this rapid lengthening of the flower stems so the wind may scatter the seeds far and wide, and doubt the providence of God if you can.

The flowers show a creamy, pale yellow in the forest, darker colors and strong green leaves in the swamps, deep yellow and thrifty around the fields, over every hill, and in every hollow. Dandelions creep into gardens and barn lots, and bloom along the roads to the very wheel tracks, everywhere developing as their environment will allow; but wherever placed, by some miracle making sufficient growth to mature a golden head and perpetuate their family. Just this yellow of dandelion is the most beautiful color in all the world. It is like strong sunshine, without which our world soon would congeal. Perhaps it is the color God loves best, for He has made the most of His flowers yellow. And He so has arranged the procession that it marches through the season dominating other colors wherever it goes, and it travels everywhere.

Yellow covers the breast of earth in dainty sorrel, violets, six or seven species of cinquefoil, and adder's tongue. It lifts its gold banner high in orchis, crested and fringed; ladies' tresses, and lady's slippers. It waves high in the well-known saffron, mullein, goldenrod of many varieties, sev-

Music of the Wild

eral marigolds, and foxglove. At half that height glow buttercups, cowslips, black-eyed susans, beg-gar's lice, snapdragons, jewel flowers, and touch-me-nots. There are several yellow lilies of the field and two of the water. Large spaces are covered with wild mustard, while sunflowers and tansy grow all along the roadside.

The Gold of God

Then there is the less-known water plantain and crowfoot, several poppies, and golden cory-dalis, two species of water cress, saxifrage, and goat's beard. There is yellow avens, wild indigo, rattle-box, and at least two varieties of clover. Also wild senna, partridge pea, yellow flax, and yellow mallow. There must be a dozen species of St. John's-wort; and frostweed, seedbox, and sundrops. That is an exquisite name, and should be applied to all yellow flowers, to indicate that the sun has dropped of her gold to paint their faces. There are several differing parsnips and loose strife. Also butterfly weed, which seems a contradiction of terms; toad flax, yellow rattle, wild honeysuckle, yellow asters, elecampane, and artichoke to end with, in the fear of growing tiresome; but this is not nearly a complete list of the gold of God, for it does not even touch the rarest exhibition that He gives.

This comes at the time of the blooming of the forest, in the mist and shimmer of early spring. Then every tree that bears nut, berry, or seed

174

FIELD DAISIES

Where the daisies march in white procession down the hill,
And the notes of the bubbling bobolink are never still.

blooms profusely. These flowers, as a rule, are not attractive singly. They are a little golden-green cluster or a fringe something like a willow catkin in shape, only longer, and each is covered with such tiny blooms so thickly placed that it requires a glass to analyze them correctly. A single bloom or a bunch of bloom or a branch is not much; but an entire forest—no, more than that—a world of it, is a different matter. When the Trees Bloom

This bloom comes at a time when our sense of color is sated with the grays and whites of winter and our lungs are starved with the stuffy artificial heating of most of our homes. It opens when the season is breaking and our hearts are mellowed with the change. The trees flower when the leaves are just beginning to unfold. Few of them are an inch long, and they are nearly as bright with yellow, pink, and silvery white as they are with green; and all their green is more strongly tinged with yellow at that time than ever again until they change color in the fall.

So when all the trees of earth are covered sparsely with golden-green leaves, and hung closely with bloom of gold, powdered deeply with dust of gold, the color is in the very air. All the world is sprinkled with it. If from some elevation you can reach a level with the top of the forest you will behold a sea of gold washing gently under waves of enchanted air, for the touch of ice still lingers, and it is perfumed with the pungent fragrance of these blossoms. Then the dormant bees awake and come pouring from hollow tree and hive to their great festival. No insects are playing or singing to rival the swarming gold and black performers; the birds have not yet returned to drown undulant humming with floods of song. The "little busy bee" comes down to the footlights and captures an appreciative audience. But the bee cares nothing for the generous applause that always greets his first appearance. Dishevelled with backing from flower clusters, his head and wings powdered with gold, his burden-bearing legs high piled with gold, he goes humming on his way. If there is anything in the idea of coloration by association, he appears to be striped with the darkness of his hollow-tree home and the gold of the pollen in which he constantly immerses himself. His mumbling, humming bumble opens the great song festival of the fields.

After a day or two, when the blossoms are ripe, the pollen dust loosens. It sifts over the fields, burnishes the breast of lake and pond with a sheet of gold, and sails on the surface of the river. Throughout the summer season nature revels in gold, but now it submerges her. She is covered from head to foot. She breathes it, she bathes in it. No wonder the coats of the bees that live upon pollen are striped with it! So beneficent is the in-

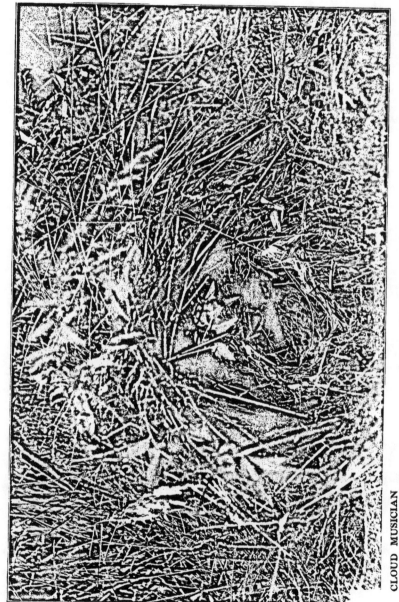

CLOUD MUSICIAN

"The mother lark that is brooding
Feels the sun on her wings,
And the deeps of the noonday glitter
With swarms of fairy things."
—Taylor.

Songs of the Fields

fluence of this gold bath that all creation has become intoxicated with it for centuries. Poets sing it, artists paint it, and natural historians wrestle with it—thus.

It appeals to me that this would be a fine time to celebrate the New Year. Why should we call the first of January the "New Year?" There is The New New-Year nothing new about a continuation of the same dead, shut-in winter season. Why go around crying, "Happy New Year!" when nothing is new and people are least happy of all their lives?

But when winter flees at the awakening of spring, when March winds arouse us, when earth thrusts up tender growth to signal us that she is ready for seed-bearing, when nature is given a new robe, the sky pure air; when the birds come home, animals creep from hibernation, and the Almighty showers His gold,—everything is refreshed, even the oldest hearts of us. Just for the sake of consistency the year should be new when the earth awakens, when human as well as bird, insect, and animal hearts are glad, when the soul is uplifted, when for a few days all nature is rich enough literally to bathe in gold.

Among the few musicians that have arrived at this time in birdland the skylark soars pre-eminent. Not that he is more beautiful than his fellows, although he comes in time to stripe his head and cover his heart with the choicest of the gold. The

181

brightness of his crown is emphasized by alter-
nating dark stripes, and his breastplate becomes
Cloud radiant in contrast with a dark collar. His back
Musicians covering is a mixture of dark-brown, gray, and
gray-brown. The wings are the same, touched with
white, and the middle feathers of the tail are sim-
ilar, the shorter outer ones tipped with white. His
habitat appears to be heaven, and his home earth,
which certainly seems contradictory. But it is true.
He is a bird of as constant flight as the kingfisher,
and of such exalted height that he is often lost to
our vision above the clouds. The kingfisher sel-
dom rises above the treetops, the lark scarcely ever
falls below. He is the oracle of high places, and
sings from greater altitude than any other bird.
That very fact may give distinction to him.

His notes, syllabicated as well as possible in
the words that of all others seem most appropriate,
"Spring o' ye-ar!" is the best-loved bird-song in
our country, and the more he slurs it and rings in
the half plaintive tone that characterizes it, the
more it is appreciated. There is a lark out in the
center of this country that greatly surpasses ours
in song, although it appears and acts very similar.
The difference in the character of the notes is detected instantly by travelers. The bird of the Ne-
braska alfalfa fields has the same slurring modu-
lations, but his song is several measures longer.
He sings, "Come here! Spring o' ye-ar!" and

ELECAMPANE

Its thrifty stalks thrust high their heads,
Flowers of pale gold to flourish.
Its roots sink deeply into earth,
Large, blue-green leaves to nourish.

Songs of the Fields

sometimes that is all of the melody, and again he adds, as if in afterthought, "My de-ar!"

Certain it is that the lark is not the greatest musician. In pure, serene, soul-piercing melody the hermit thrush surpasses him; also the wood robin, brown thrush, mocking-bird, and several others. Nevertheless to half the people of earth the lark is the sweetest of bird songsters. There must be a reason, for his notes will not compare with many rivals; so one must look elsewhere for the source of his popularity.

For one thing, while doves and bluebirds arrive as early, his is the first universal song our longing ears hear in the spring. There are times when to be first in the field is half the battle. He is trailing his notes, clear and easily syllabicated, back and forth across heaven, over town and village, and even above great cities, before any other bird is heard, unless, indeed, you except the cry of the killdeer. Then his soring propensity, the fact that he drops a note from above cloud, gives ground for the belief that he picked it up there. If a canvass were made of the people of earth as to their favorite bird, it is sure that a large majority of them would vote for the lark. That this preference is founded on sentiment rather than fact has nothing to do with the case. Because he is common, friendly, and sings first and nearest heaven, he is the bird of the people. Neither does

185

the fact that not one-tenth of these same lark-lovers ever heard the song of the hermit thrush have anything to do with the case. They prefer the lark because they so love him they are convinced they yet would like him best if they did hear the thrush.

From their choir-loft one would suppose that elms were not high enough to furnish larks a nesting-place. That is the great surprise about them. **Earth-born Singers** Because he whistles close earth, and brings forth his young on its breast, the quail seems consistent. Because the lark sings nearest heaven one would expect him to have the nesting habits of the wood pewee. But he drops abruptly to earth, *bare* earth, and in the shelter of a grassy hummock or amidst the growing clover or wheat establishes a home. His mate turns on the point of her breast until she wears out a hollow that she lines, and often roofs, with dry grasses, leaving her door to the east, in most instances, as my observation has proved. From four to six eggs are deposited—more often six — and almost always the brood comes off safely.

Larks are secretive and shy about their building. They always walk several yards under cover of the grasses on leaving their nests before they take wing, and return to them in the same manner, so that when you see a lark alight you are not sure he is within a rod of his home in any di-

THE HOME OF THE HOP-TOAD

Nestled by my cabin's damp stone wall
Where wild rose petals softly fall,
Old Hop-Toad sleeps throughout the day,
But at night he's a hunter, alert and gay.

rection. Because they are accustomed to seeing only open, level meadow it is very difficult to place a camera close or win their confidence sufficiently to be able to make studies of them. Every brooding song-bird sits on the point of the breast, and where an arched cup also raises the long tail the mother has a cramped, spread-out appearance. This one brooded on six eggs and brought off her young safely.

There is a shade of yellow on the breast of a young lark when it takes wing, that has escaped commerce, and it is infinitely more delicate and beautiful than the nearest approach to it. There is another exquisite yellow, not yet in use, on the face of a freshly opened false foxglove, and another on unclosing buckeye buds. An unusual yellow can be found in the bloom of elecampane. Four New Yellows

This magnificent plant grows from five to six feet high, in big round stems, having long, hairy, blue-green leaves of a frosty appearance, that surround the stem at their base and curve off gracefully to the tip. The flower has a round head, with irregular, straggling petals of beautiful yellow that harmonize exquisitely with the leaves. Here is another plant that I am sure the artists of Japan do not know, else before this all of us would have become familiar with it in screen decorations. I can recall no statelier growth, no leaf form more impressive.

Music of the Wild

In my home all my literary and artistic efforts have a critic; the keenest they ever know: one who cuts to the bone and spares not. She **My Critic** is actuated solely by love. Being sensitive to criticisms from other sources, she would point out all the flaws in my work herself, and so prevent others from seeing them too late to be avoided.

"You never are going to put in that hop-toad!" she exclaims.

"Why not?"

"Because this is a music-book, and the song of a hop-toad is not worth mentioning."

"Well, if it can not sing much it can set a poet singing, which amounts to the same thing. Listen!"—

" Howdy, Mister Hop-Toad! Glad to see you out!
Bin a month o' Sundays sence I see you hereabout.

Mister Hop-Toad, honest-true-Springtime—don't you love it?
You old rusty rascal you, at the bottom of it!

Swell that fat old throat o' yourn and lemme see you swaller;
Straighten up and h'ist your head! You don't owe a dollar!

Hulk, sulk, and blink away, you old bloat-eyed rowdy!
Hain't you got a word to say? Won't you tell me howdy?''

Why should a hop-toad have a voice, or strain **The Song** his throat, when he can compel a poet to sing for **of the** **Hop-Toad** him like that? Burns sang for a louse and a field mouse, Bryant for a mosquito, Emerson for the

190

HOP-TOAD

"Mr. Hop-Toad, honest true—Springtime—don't you love it?
You old rusty rascal you, at the bottom of it!"
                                            —*Riley.*

bumblebee; the poet who put the snail into met-
rical measure preferred to remain anonymous, and
other writers have ranged through nature and
lifted their voices for almost every living creature;
but when our own Riley brought every reader of
his lines down to earth and in harmony with a hop-
toad, he sang the greatest song of all, for they
occupy a place with humanity set aside for cater-
pillars, snakes, and bats. From time immemorial
men have shuddered on seeing a toad. In connec-
tion with it such pleasing fiction has been culti-
vated as that to touch one would develop warts on
your fingers and make your cow give bloody milk.
Also they were a component part of the brews
compounded by witches.

These silly superstitions, passed from genera-
tion to generation, were splendid protection to the
toad. Let it alone! Who wanted warts on his fin-
gers and blood in his milk? You may be very
sure it was left alone. "It's a toad! Don't touch
it!" rang the cry.

So the hop-toad homes in the bushes and un-
der the vines, sleeping during the heat of the day,
and coming out in the evening for his food. He
consumes untold numbers of gnats, mosquitoes,
small flies, fireflies, and tiny worms on grass blades.
The home that boasts a hop-toad is particularly
fortunate, for he is a great scavenger, and his wel-
come should be hearty. For years we have had

Music of the Wild

one that lived throughout the summer season among the rosebushes along the line fence west of the cabin, and no doubt hibernated somewhere on the premises. This past summer the same one, or another similar, moved around to the orchard and slept among some sunflowers and wild roses shading my bedroom window. My critic found him, and came racing to know if I wanted his picture, but later she objected to having it used in this book. The poem reconstructed her, as it should every one.

You will find it in complete form in the "Home Folk's" volume of Riley's poems, and if you do not own the book, get it at once and learn what you have missed. As has been explained, the hoptoad is one of our home folks and lives very close, within a few feet of us, and works as diligently for our comfort as the martins of the windmill, that, with bats and flycatchers, clear the air overhead of insect pests.

There is perpetual amazement in the amount of natural history a poet knows. Does he make **What** an especial study of it or does he see so clearly **Poets** that an object is photographed on his brain and **Know** he writes of it without knowing that he has impoverished the text-books? Take this poem by James Whitcomb Riley. It is a song of three stanzas, with a uniform refrain to each. From it you learn the fact that the toad has hibernated; the season of his appearance, his location, and his character-

194

MOONSEED VINE

We plant and trim and train our vines,
Shaping them into wondrous designs;
But God's go sprawling wild and free,
Over wayside fence and tree.

Songs of the Fields

istics. In personal appearance, you are told that
he has a rusty back, a habit of ducking his head,
a full throat, the palpitant motion of which is
touched upon, as are his warts, and his "bloat"
eyes; while in the question, "S'pose I want to 'flict
you any more 'an what you air?" is encompassed
a volume on his social status.

I wish that every person in the world were com-
pelled to read this poem in order to attain a ra-
tional attitude concerning so valuable a friend and
neighbor as the hop-toad, in the first place; and in
the second, to come to a realization of the things
that lie at the bottom of the bubbling fountain in
the heart of a poet. I have had undisputed pos-
session of all the hop-toads in my vicinity since
my birth; so the feeling that I had been patted
on the head and personally commended came to
me on first reading this exquisite song.

Every grain field of earth has its choral union,
but it long has been a study of mine to decide which
musicians have the loveliest environment. I was **My Oat-**
strongly attracted with wheat; corn, rye, buck- **Field**
wheat, all had weighty consideration, and clover
almost tipped the scales of my judgment in its
favor, but after years of deliberation the choice
has fallen on oats. This decision rests solely on
artistic merit. The market value of a subject that
furnishes me a picture or sings me a song is of
no consideration. Is it beautiful? Does it touch

197

Music of the Wild

the heart? Does it stir the imagination and force expression to the lips? If so, it is past monetary value.

We are not dealing with model farms, and so in the beginning the upturned earth of my oat field Moon- is beautiful, because at the heels of the plowman seed on follow larks, blackbirds, bluebirds, and robins pick-a Snake Fence ing grubs; and the warm spring air is vibrant with their notes. The field is enclosed by a straggling old snake-fence overgrown with carrion vine and moonseed; the corners filled with alder, wild rose, milkweed, saffron, and wild mustard, and inter-laced with dodder in myriads of fine gold threads. There are big forest trees all around it, making a hedge reaching heavenward. Every insect and bird of the field homes there, and the river sing-ing along on one side adds not only its voice, but the notes of kingfisher, killdeer, sheilpoke, and sandpiper.

From a few inches in height the growing oats show a rare blue-green color with frosty lights, seen in no other grain. When the lacy heads are almost matured, and nodding "Good-day" to the level rays of the setting sun, and bowing "Good-evening" to the white lights of the rising moon; when one at a time thousands of fireflies rise from earth, light their lanterns, and begin the business of life; when numberless insects play or sing; when the big trees rock softly, cradling sleeping

198

MY OAT-FIELD

When the foxfire burns beside the river,
The crickets sing under tawny leaves,
And grasshopper fiddles solemnly quiver,
While the harvesters gather the sheaves.

Songs of the Fields

birds, and the river whispers their lullaby,—the oat
field is the most beautiful on God's footstool, and
it is alive with musicians.

A few days later, when blue tints give place
to the gold of approaching ripeness, it is lovely
in a warm, mellow way. Because there is unlim-
ited sameness in a field of growing grain a pho-
tographic study of it is not pleasing. The time
to reproduce it is when the cutting is over and
the harvest stands in shocks, from the canopy of
which crickets sing, a million in unison. Locusts
hum in the big trees, wild doves coo from the
thicket across the river, the clacking reaper rattles
a rhythmic accompaniment, and my partners,
bending over the sheaves, touch the scene with
life and color. I never see harvesters cutting
grain that I do not think of a command uttered
by Moses three thousand years ago: "And when
ye reap the harvest of your land, thou shalt not
wholly reap the corners of thy field, neither shalt
thou gather the gleanings of the harvest." Moses
intended these gleanings to remain for the "poor
and the stranger." In my country gleanings fall
to the birds, since these fields know neither the
poor nor the stranger. Harvesting scenes are so
touched with life, music, and color that they al-
ways have been great favorites with artists and
poets. The most vivid shirt of a workman or
the red 'kerchief knotted around his throat is not

so brilliant, however, as the pageant of color
marching adown the old snake-fence.

To the whites of alder and the pink of wild
rose are added the lavender of beard's tongue,
Wild the blue of bellflower, nodding plumy heads of
Lilies meadow rue, and, scattered here and there, wild
tiger lilies. These bear the palm for brilliant color.
The flowers are so artistic that decorators almost
have worn them out for art purposes, and yet no
one has reproduced them with all the beauty of
one wild bed I know.

These lilies grow in rather damp, sandy places,
sometimes in real swamp, sometimes on land that
would seem too high and dry for them. They
have brilliant orange-red faces, thickly freckled
with brown. The bud is a long point, the half-
unfolded bloom a trumpet, the full-blown flower
curls its petals so far back it almost turns inside
out and fully displays the grace of the long sta-
mens and pistil. In damp ground the flower color
is paler, and the stems and buds longer. They
are of deeper red and lower growth in dry loca-
tions; but in half moist, half sandy soil they reach
perfection.

For three years from passing railroad trains
A Moving I had seen the finest bed of these lilies of all my
Flower-bed experience, on land owned by the company, just
inside the fence enclosing rather deep woods, a
mile or two below the village of Ceylon, beside the

" BRANDS OF THE NOONTIDE BEAM "

"The lily with the sprinkled dots,
Brands of the moontide beam;
The cardinal, and the blood-red spots,
Its double in the stream." —Holmes.

Songs of the Fields

Long farm. This season, when a study of them was wanted in their prime, the cameras were loaded, and the trip made in all confidence—not a lily was to be found, nor the ghost of a lily. Even more, the embankment next the woods was cut away at least a foot in depth, and leveled. Then began a search all over my country for a large bed of them, with no results. A week had not helped matters, when my critic came from a drive and announced that beside the railroad, half way to Bryant, was a superb growth of lilies that, she thought, was just what I wanted. She brought one for a sample, and she was not mistaken.

So great was the fear that flower hunters might gather them or railroad employees mow the land that the trip was made in the rain. A glance showed what had happened. The railroad company had cut down the embankment beside the Long farm and filled in a low place near the Limberlost crossing with the earth. In so doing they had transplanted my lilies, and greatly to the advantage of the flowers; for here they were in a moist location, and were shaded all the long, hot afternoons. As a result these lilies prove that they grew in closer clusters, taller, and with blooms very nearly twice the size of the average wild lily. After the studies were secured and the flowers were needed no longer, they peeped at me from several fence corners around the Limberlost, Can-

Music of the Wild

oper, and Valley of the Wood Robin, just beyond which lay my finest field of oats.

The bees and all kinds of flies and insects were attracted to it by the blooms along the fence; birds Grain-field Vocalists of every field family sought the insects, the berries of the bushes, and water. Lift a shock of oats, and thousands of black field crickets poured from under it. Touch any weed or swaying clover head, and a grasshopper sprang from it as if shot from a catapult, while the chorus of those scattered over the field made a constant minor to louder notes. So the oats field had more than a fair share of inhabitants, and almost without exception they were musicians that joined the choir, and sang and played incomparably.

Grasshoppers are extremely interesting. They are good-natured, clean, and industrious. They must be naturally musical, for they need not sing all day and half the night unless they choose. At least one would not think their notes compulsory, and the production of them appears to be work. Grasshoppers seem to be enclosed in a coat of mail, so firm and hard is the striped, glassy covering. They make music with the stiff wingshields by half raising and rubbing them at the base. The notes are a queer "Zerrrrrrrrrrrrrrr" of a sound, increasing in volume for a few seconds, and then falling away in three slow, distinct notes, "Tink, tink, tink."

206

THE LANDLORD OF THE FIELDS

"Thou dost drink and dance and sing,
Happier than the happiest king!

Songs of the Fields

They are cleanly, else they would not be wash-
ing forever. It almost appears at times as if they
must carry a Lady Macbeth curse, that they try
to wash away. They wash their antennæ, heads,
bodies, wings, each of their four small feet, and
then the long, springboard legs and larger feet.
After a few bites of pollen, plant-juice, or any
dead insects upon which they may happen, they
wash again. They are the genuine "water babies"
of the fields, and the most insistent musicians.
Sometimes they like the open fields, but a little
search among the grasses and flowers around the
old snake-fences will prove hoppers even more nu-
merous there. This may be because the rails and
bushes afford protection from bird enemies.

The unusually wet season of 1907 did many
queer things afield, none more amazing than the
growth it made possible among some flowers of
low habit. Botanists tell you that beard-tongue
(Pentstemon pubescens) grows from one foot to
a foot and a third. At that height to the casual
observer it is almost lost among the grasses and
undergrowth. This season many people called
my attention to a delicately colored, lacy, exquisite
flower they never before had seen. It was beard-
tongue, growing all through the Limberlost, along
Canoper way, in Rainbow Bottom, and around the
fields, to the height of the top of seven-rail fences.
It sprang up a smooth, thrifty stalk, grew slender

Music of the Wild

green leaves, and unusually large pale lavender flowers of much grace and beauty.

The blooms are a trumpet-shaped corolla, with two escallops turning up and three down. There **Beard-** is a stamen, covered with long hairs, and fertilized **tongue** by the pollen it gathers from the down of visiting butterflies and bees. From this organ the plant takes its name, beard-tongue. Many people unacquainted with a natural growth gathered and were enthusiastic over it at the height of a fence. It was very beautiful bordering grain fields, nowhere more so than around the oats where this study was made.

While birds and insects hover over these old snake-fences, the squirrels race along them and frightened cotton-tails sail between the rails like skilled acrobats. Rabbits burrow their nests in grain fields and pastures, and beside the fences under the cover of bottom rails and stumps of dead trees. Close harvest time their young appear. Mere youth and helplessness make its appeal. The nestlings of song birds are ugly, naked little creatures, blind, and agape. But again, some ground builders—the quail, rail, and many water birds—are able to travel on leaving their shells, and are irresistible balls of fluff. Newly-born rabbits and squirrels are blind and unattractive, but when led forth to support themselves are beautiful and trustingly innocent. A few days' contact with the

210

BEARD-TONGUE

"There's beard on your tongue!" laughed the lily,
As she tossed her head with wild grace.

Songs of the Fields

world teaches them so many painful lessons they become wild and shy as their elders.

When this young cotton-tail no longer felt the need of the blanket his mother had raked her sides to furnish, he trustingly came out to the big world and on a strip of bank posed for many studies. He greedily nibbled leaves, washed his face when he finished, with all the care of a grass-hopper, and then stretched himself for a sunbath. When his pictures were taken he was put with the remainder of his family at the edge of the oats. It must be that rabbits escape their natural enemies with much skill, or else they breed in untold numbers, for every fall and winter men slaughter them without mercy, and each succeeding fall they seem to be quite as numerous.

Hunters say that despite speed in running they are silly creatures, and often sit perfectly still, trusting to the resemblance of their fur to surrounding dry grass and weeds to protect them, until they are killed. Not being a hunter, I can tell little about these animals when pursued. If hunted with a camera that is concealed and focused on the mouth of their burrow, and a few apples, pieces of cabbage or carrots, of which they are especially fond, left around, they tame rapidly and take many interesting poses. It is doubtful if there is anything so wild that it is not susceptible to judicions friendly advances. We read in the Book of

Molly Cotton

213

Music of the Wild

James, "For *every* kind of beasts, and of birds, and of serpents, and of things in the sea, is tamed, and hath been tamed of mankind."

In most cases this word "tamed" should be changed to "broken." When birds and beasts are Caging the Wild trapped in their wild estate, caged and starved or beaten into non-resistance or through familiarity endure the presence of men without signs of fear, they are said to be "tamed." In fact, they are heart-broken for home, starving for natural diet, and crazed for lack of space, so that they are slowly dying, and too desolate to resist. Think of a bird that has ranged the heavens from Canada to Patagonia reduced to the hop from perch to perch and the folded wing estate of a two by three foot cage—and that is considered unusually large. Or of a beast that has roamed the forest and marsh for miles being confined inside bars where it can not turn without touching steel. Is it any wonder these "tamed" creatures kill when they have opportunity? Our laws provide for the taming of "wild" men in the same manner, and it is noticeable that they, too, kill at the slightest chance for escape, if they do not lose their reason and murder the first person they meet.

There is a shrub frequenting many of my fence corners that has escaped art and that decorators do not know. I think it has great possibilities. It grows to the average height of fence-corner

214

MOLLY COTTON

"After lunch I wash my face
And go to have a romp
With other little Cotton-tails
Down in the Limberlost Swamp."

Songs of the Fields

shrubs such as papaw and alder, and, if it had opportunity, no doubt would make a medium-sized tree. The stems are smooth and round, quite deeply indented in places with the strain of growth. The leaves are large, nobly shaped, and variable in shades of color; rather thick for a leaf, and pulpy. The blooms are little clusters of white florets, not at all remarkable. The Burning Bush

The shrub takes its name from the seed pods. These pods are scattered sparsely over a bush, hang from long, graceful stems, and are divided into three or four sections, the shape of which can be seen in the picture, the color coral-pink. Each of these thirds or quarters, as the case may be, contains a seed. When the seed is ripe the section opens, forcing the triangles apart and displaying the flame-colored inside. This interior color is the crowning glory and beauty of the bush, for which it is named. There is no doubt at all but the scientist who classified it thought of Moses and the "burning bush," and so gave that name to the shrub.

This burning bush, to my knowledge, flourishes in half a dozen different soils and locations, making me believe it would be particularly adaptive for lawn ornamentation. These seed pods cling after the leaves fall, and give a touch of brilliant color to their location that would be particularly appreciated, for most of the bushes we buy of our

217

Music of the Wild

florists are a cluster of bare twigs in winter. When
the pods open, the membranes incasing the seed
are bright carmine, exactly the shade of the inner
lining of *Ebonymus Americanus*.

The shrubs and bushes beside these old fences
are tenanted from leaf to ground with life, and
a volume of sound arises constantly from earth in
the summer time. The clearest enunciator and the
handsomest insect of all is the katy-did. What a
very, very delightful thing it must have been that
Katy did! How her descendants rejoice in telling
it over and over. It of necessity had to be some-
thing wonderfully fine. In all the world there is
not enough rancor to sing of an evil deed adown
all time since the morning of creation. But this
charming thing that Katy did has been celebrated
from the beginning, and will be to the end. Surely
it was something big and broad, beneficial to all
her race, and the wide world as well—else why are
her minstrels forever celebrating her act? It had
to be something obvious, too; for while they con-
stantly affirm the deed, they never specify just
what was done, and this neglect must arise from
the fact that they suppose all of us know. I be-
lieve Katy was the first of her family to discover
sound and teach all of her relatives to voice the
fullness of their joy in life on their fiddles in such
exquisite measure and inflection that they deceive
most of us into thinking it song. To have given

**What did
Katy do?**

218

BURNING BUSH

They thought how the Lord spoke to Moses,
When they saw its glowing flame,
And so they said to each other,
"Burning bush" shall be its name.

to her kin their medium of self-expression, that would have entitled Katy to the immortality she has earned.

"Katy did!" triumphs one of her admirers, as if it were a fact just discovered.

"Katy did it!" emphasizes another worshiper.

"Katy did!" corroborates a friend in the next bush.

"Katy did it!" iterates the first, with all assurance; and the manner in which these exquisite insects can emphasize their notes is marvelous. Not a bird of ornithology can speak plainer, better-accented English than they, not even the whip-poor-will; and no insects can approach them. Compared with their clean-cut, distinctly enunciated syllables, all the remainder of their insect relatives are mere scrapers, buzzers, and hummers.

The remarkable thing about it is that the speech is made by the contact of the glassy plates **How** at the base of the wings, and in much the same **Katy did it** manner as the grasshopper produces his strident buzz. Because the fields seem to be the true home of the katy-did does not prevent the family from scattering widely. There are a few in the forest, many in the marshes, and from the fields they come close country homes. Most of their music is made in August and September, when they are matured, mating, and depositing their eggs.

No insect of their species is so beautiful as

they. The adult is a solid green of pale color, yellowish in faint tints in some lights, a dainty bluish **Katy's** in others. The faceplate and wide "choker" ap- **Costume** pear to be of the same glassy coat of mail as those of the grasshopper. The legs are very long, and the hind pair has claspers. The wings resemble deeply veined and grooved leaves, the musical plates showing at the bases. The insect is very narrow of body, but quite deep, and the back and abdomen are sharp ridges. The antennæ are almost twice the length of the body, and so hair-fine that a camera focused on a katy-did does not record their full extent. With these they explore their path, lightly touching objects before them to find footing and avoid danger. Their greatest protection lies in their close resemblance to tender green leaves.

They have what appears to be a stubby little tail turning up at the back. This is the instrument with which they insert their eggs between the layers of a green leaf in the fall. The leaf drops, and lies during the winter, and the next summer the egg develops into a tiny katy-did, that emerges and sets to work foraging on the under side of foliage. All that is accomplished by growth in this insect is to become larger, as they are always shaped much the same; possibly the young ones are of a more tender, yellowish green, that changes to a bluish cast as they reach maturity.

TALL MEADOW RUE

Of all the roadside flowers that bloom
The old snake fence to hide,
Tall meadow rue is the joy of June,
Its lacy, graceful bride.

Songs of the Fields

Katy-dids are immaculately clean, dainty insects. No other member of the "hopper" group moves with such calm deliberation. They have all the time there is, and seem to know it. They never hurry and are wholly lacking in the nervous energy of the grasshopper, cricket, and locust. So very deliberate are they that there is a possibility, fostered by their constant wetting of the feet with a mucus they eject, that walking is a difficult matter for them, and one to be accomplished only with great caution. To my mind the katy-did is the handsomest, the best musician, and the most interesting of all insects anywhere near its family.

From the frequent overflowing of the river, that not only decays but washes away rails, one side of my oat field is profaned by a short stretch of wire fence. This is to be forgiven only because, as can be seen so clearly, it is necessary. Then, too, it is in such a damp, shaded place that no harm whatever results. The vines and bushes almost cover the wire, and queer long-legged water birds tilt and rock when they try to perch on it. Where it escapes the river the old rail fence still stands, and every year clothes it with richer beauty and brings it—alas! like all the remainder of the world—nearer the end. _{The Snake Fence}

I have cause for quarrel with scientists who named many of our flowers and vines. It seems at times as if they tried themselves, as witness:

Music of the Wild

monkey flower, butterfly *weed,* jewel*weed, toad*-flax, and *carrion* vine. Of all the decorations that

Incongruous Flower Names entwine these old fences none is more beautiful than the carrion vine. But what a name! Enough to prejudice any one. All because the ball of greenish-yellow bloom has a faint pungent odor that impressed Linnæus, or some other early writer, as slightly disagreeable. It can not be so very noxious, either, for the bees should know their business, and they gather its pollen eagerly. God put that pungent, almost sour odor in some flowers to cut the cloying sweetness of others, and make honey edible.

So this beautiful vine is disgraced, and there are so many more appropriate names it might have borne quite as well. It is difficult to understand why a slightly unusual odor of the flower should have been emphasized, while the exquisite cutting and texture of the leaves is overlooked. They are heart-shaped at the base, curving off to a long lance-point, of delicate texture, and of lovely shades of green that vary as the light falls on them. So why not name it "lance leaf" or "golden globe," either of which is quite as appropriate as carrion vine and not suggestive of anything objectionable.

Another common, but peculiar vine of my territory is wild yam, the dried seed pods of which form nature's best rattlebox. *Dioscorea villosa* is a great beauty. Its leaves are a perfect heart-

226

shape as a heart is conventionalized, and so deeply veined that their golden-green surfaces catch the light in hills and hollows. Where the vine grows in bright sunlight along the road these leaves are so closely set they overlap like the scales on a fish. Its bloom is insignificant, the male flowers drooping clusters, the female spike-like heads. The seeds are small triangles, and a number of them are placed on a long stem. When these are dry and shaken by winter winds they make as good music as the hop tree.

Another old snake fence corner pet of mine, that flourishes in cultivation, and that is dignified and an artistic plant, is wild saffron. It bears **Wild** transplanting well, and if its location and soil are **Saffron** at all congenial, in a few years it grows into a most attractive bush. It reaches from three to four feet in height, many shoots upspringing from the same root. The stems are round, smooth, and even, with a slight yellow tint to their green, that extends to the leaves also. These are set at different places, and point in all directions. They are very graceful, as each is made up of twenty small leaves set on a midrib. Approaching the top, the last nine or ten have a small spray of bloom branching from their bases.

These little bloom-sprays and the large crown of the plant are masses of small individual yellow flowers having five cuppy petals of unequal length, and anthers so dark-brown as to be mistaken for black at a casual glance. Both the leaves and the bloom-clusters help to give it a delicate, lacy appearance. I can not so describe the flowers as to paint an adequate idea of their richness. The separate sprays at the leaf bases appear lighter yellow than the massive head and show the individual flowers better. The crown is a conical mist of gold accented by touches of almost black. Saffron is a stately and distinguished plant of great beauty in the fence corners, where it has a struggle to preserve its individuality among the masses of growth around it. On a lawn its every feature of distinction would be enhanced.

One point that should be of especial interest to those who wish to try the cultivation of wild flowers and trees on their premises, is the range of color in the mid-summer and fall species. Many people relying on cultivated shrubs and flowers grow a mass of spring and early summer bloom, and have bare shrubs and leafless vines in fall and winter. The field flowers are a blaze of color all summer until frost, and there are several vines, bushes, and trees that are brilliant with seeds and berries throughout the winter.

Few words of our language are more suggestive of peace and comfort than "pasture." *Pasto-rem,* a green feeding-ground, according to the old Latins. And wherever there is a green feeding-

Green Pastures

GREEN PASTURES

"He maketh me to lie down in green pastures"
Like the cattle on daisy-flecked hill,
He leadeth me gently toward Him,
Beside the waters so still.

ground you may be very sure you will find the shade of trees and bushes, and frequently there is running water. Wherever you locate these you hear a swelling bird and insect chorus. From the dawn of history men in travel and in burden-bearing have been very dependent on their beasts, and so have sought to make suitable provision for them. This setting off a space of growing food for stock is without date, and over and over the chroniclers of the Bible made use of the comparison of the care of men for their flocks with the care of God for men.

"The Lord is my Shepherd; I shall not want. He maketh me to lie down in green pastures; He leadeth me beside the still waters."

The bodily comfort we give to our beasts made the basis of a comparison with the spiritual comfort God gives us, in one of the most beautiful expressions ever portrayed in language, "He maketh me to lie down in green pastures." Before the eye rises the picture of a lush, green meadow sprinkled with daisies and dotted with buttercups; the lark overhead, and the full-fed cattle lying—pictures of contentment in the shade of the newly-leafing trees that ring with the songs of courting birds. The thought of a pasture is in some way connected with spring; perhaps because, as at no other time, the cattle cry for it, and beg piteously to be released to natural food. At that time the pastures are green; later they may not be. Then

Music of the Wild

the cattle, dry-fed during the long winter, graze
and graze until they become so fat the milk they
give grows richer, and housewives make what they
call "clover" butter.

When man treats the beasts that sustain and
enrich him with the consideration he would like
were he a beast, we have one of the very highest
signs of the grace of God in the human heart.
This study was made at almost four o'clock in the
afternoon, when the cattle, after a day of grazing,
were lying in fullfed content. It was so early in
the season that hickory and late-leafing trees were
bare, but already the stock sought for their resting-
place the *shade* afforded by maple and elms.

There was no real necessity for shelter. The
heat was not sufficient to worry them, but the in-
clination to lie in the shade was instinctive. Scat-
tered around this pasture and in almost every
fence corner there grows a tree for the express pur-
pose of providing comfort for the stock and a
choir-loft for field musicians. How the cattle ap-
preciate this can be seen by their gathering to lie
in the strip of light shade in the early spring! If
they seek a sheltered spot when they really do not
need it, what would become of them in the burn-
ing heat of July and August without it? How
the birds love it they tell you in their notes of
bubbling ecstasy.

Not far from this pasture are the grazing lands

A Sign
of God in
the Heart

SHELTERED, WATERED PASTURE

"I envy the stream, as it glides along
Through its beautiful banks in a trance of song."
—Bryant.

Songs of the Fields

of some "progressive" farmers. These fields are enclosed in straight wire fences, guiltless of a leaf for shelter, so they offer migrant musicians no in- ducement to locate there. All the season tortured horses and cattle graze in early morning and evening, and at noontime stand in restless groups, striving to drive away the flies, and find shelter from each other's bodies; for neither cattle nor horses lie when they have finished grazing unless there is shade. To rest in the open would be to place themselves between two fires—the reflected heat from the earth and the direct heat from the sun.

"He maketh me to lie down in green pastures," I quoted, when passing such a field on a scorching August day.

"He sendeth His rain to the just as well as to the unjust," quoted my critic, in reply. "You know if I were He, I would not. I would send rain only to pastures with trees in them, and burn all the remainder."

So we agreed to keep watch as we drove across the country, making these illustrations, and see how much we could learn of the disposition of the farmers by the manner in which they provided for their stock and their birds. Soon it became apparent that the man who stripped a pasture of every tree treated his family with no greater consideration. There was scarcely a tree anywhere on his premises. In one place we counted four big

237

Music of the Wild

stumps, all within a few rods of the house that the felled trees had shaded from noon until sunset. These trees had been cut within the past two years, and the house had stood for many. There was not a growth anywhere around it except a few scrub cedars, and not a bird note. It was bared to the burning heat.

What would it have meant to the women and children of that stopping-place, for there was no A Road- sign of home around it, to have had the tight pal-side Dream ing-fence torn away from the few yards immediately surrounding the house; the shelter of those big trees, with an easy·seat beneath them, and a hammock swinging between? I dreamed those trees were growing again and filled with bird notes, that fence down, a coat of fresh paint on the house, the implements standing in the barn lot sheltered, and one day's work spent in arranging the premises. Into the dream would come a vision of open doors and windows, the sound of the voices of contented women, the shouts of happy children, and the chirping of many birds.

Some farms belong to men my critic calls a "tight-wad." That is not a classic expression; but if you saw the lands from which every tree had been sold, the creeks and ponds dried and plowed over, the fields inclosed in stretches of burning wire fence to allow cultivation within a few inches of it, not a bird note sounding,—you would un-

BLAZING STAR

"Every clod feels a stir of might,
An instinct within it that reaches and towers
And, blindly groping above it for light,
Climbs to a soul in grass and flowers."
                                    —Lowell.

Songs of the Fields

derstand why the term is suitable as none other.
Even if the Almighty did give the earth to the
children of men, it scarcely seems fair to Him to Nature's Gentle Men
efface every picture and hush all song. It is diffi-
cult to realize just what would happen were most
men farming by this method. But we still have
left some degree of comfort because there are so
many of nature's gentle men: men who see the
pictures, hear the songs, and wish to perpetuate
them for their children.

I know a farm that has been for three genera-
tions in the same family, passing from father to
son. The home—mark the word—is on a little hill
in the middle of the land, obscured by surround-
ing trees from the road and its dust and travel.
The quaint old house is a story and a half, and a
porch extends the length of the front and both
sides. That home even turns its back to the road.
The front porch and door face the orchard in the
center of the land, "where father always sat when
he rested, so that he could hear the birds and bees
sing," the son told me.

There are old beehives under the trees, and the
grass is long and fine. One could look at that
orchard in mid-winter and tell to a certainty just
what music would swell there in June. The blue-
bird would claim the hollow apple tree, the catbird
the plum thicket, the robin, jay, and dove the ap-
ple trees, and the ground sparrow the earth. The

hens would mother broods there, the turkeys slip around warily, and the guineas clatter in the grass. Martins and swallows homing under the barn eaves would sail above the trees, and blackbirds from the creek would build on high branches. But no dream could encompass all the music that would swell there throughout the summer.

Any lover of sunshine, bird song, and orchard pictures almost could see the old man who finished his day's work and then rested himself with music, sitting beneath his trees, worshiping God in nature. I have known many men like him, and all of them had bodies as strong as their trees, music in their hearts if the birds failed to sing, and faces serene as summer skies.

The garden lies on one side of the dooryard, the barn lot on the other. The garden is a quaint **An Old-** commingling of use and beauty. There are rasp-**fashioned** berry, currant, and gooseberry bushes along the **Garden** sides and across the foot, but on either hand at the front gate are flowers. Large clusters of white lilies grow by each post, and cinnamon pink, larkspur, ragged robin, and many sweet, old-fashioned blooms overflow the beds. Straight down the center is another big flower-bed, and at each side of it squares of radishes, onions, lettuce, salsify, spinach, strawberries,—everything edible, and all flower-bordered. In each corner is a peach tree, and there are others scattered here and there.

WILLOWS

"*Give fools their gold, and knaves their power;*
Let fortune's bubbles rise and fall;
Who sows a field, or trains a flower,
Or plants a tree, is more than all."
—*Whittier.*

Songs of the Fields

The dooryard is filled with pear, plum, apple, and some fine, big walnut trees. The barn is of logs; and at the door and all around the well and watering-trough are beds of crushed stone. Across the end of the house, facing the road, "father" built a schoolroom. It was fifteen feet wide and twenty long. There he taught the neighbors' children in winter and dried fruit in summer. Just back of the house a large meadow, tree-sprinkled, stretches down to the road, and in the corner next to the barn grow three willows so mighty that they called me to them,—and so I discovered a home, and "father" and "mother."

In a little dip in the meadow near the barn "father" planted those three willows thirty years ago. When they had grown to sufficient size to make enough shade, because the barn was low and hot, he built this big feed-trough under them, and then he carried corn and grain to it. The trough is six feet wide, eighteen long, and six inches deep. One of the trees is nine feet in circumference, one twelve, and one fourteen; and "all the birds of the heaven make their nests" in these boughs, while the trees sing unceasingly. The watering-trough, that father always kept filled, stands along the side of the yard fence next the barn. There must be forty acres of woods, from which trees have been taken only for fuel and to let in enough light to make the grass grow for pasture.

Comfort for Stock

245

Music of the Wild

"Father"
and
"Mother"

I never saw "father" and "mother." They were gone before the willows called me. Her son told me that "mother had big brown eyes and white hair, and her cheeks were always a little pink." Of course they were. Like the cinnamon pinks of her garden. So by the lilies and the ragged robins and her porch, facing *from* the dust and turmoil of travel, we know "mother." And by the schoolhouse he built with his hands, by the cultivation of beauty and music all around his home and entire farm, by the neatness of his barns and outbuildings, by the trees he spared and the trees he planted, we know "father." By these things we know where "father" is to-day. So when the last book is written and the last picture made, if I have done my work nearly so well as "father" did his, perhaps we will have a happy meeting.

I should love to tell him that his work lives as an example to his neighbors; how his willows have grown, and that they called me from afar, and I put them into a book for thousands to see, that they might learn of his great-hearted humanity. I shall want to tell him how many hours I have lain on the grass under the big pear tree at the corner of his house, of all the lunches I have eaten on the front porch looking into the orchard, of the cotton-tails that yet scampered there unafraid, and how one season a little red-eyed vireo built on a branch of the apple tree swaying across

BUCKEYE BRANCH

"The buds of the buckeye in spring are the first,
And the willow's gold hair then appears,
And snowy the cups of the dogwood that burst
By the red bud, with pink-tinted tears."
                                        —Fosdick.

the end of the porch just above where "mother" always sat with her mending. Heaven is heaven because it will allow me to tell "father" and "mother" these things.

One of the beautiful trees this man spared for decorative purposes was the buckeye. I wonder if it was so named from the resemblance of the The rich dark-brown nut to the eye of the deer. The Buckeye trees grow more rapidly than some others, flourishing on upland, slightly sandy soil. The buds are large and open, to display vivid streaks of red and yellow in the spring. The colors are very rich. The flower is a long tassel, covered by tiny florets of greenish yellow. The leaves are oblong, deeply veined, and grow in clusters of four to the stem.

The fruit is a round nut, encased in a pulpy hull, dotted with warts of a bright tan-yellow in the fall. The nuts and hulls sometimes drop together, and sometimes the hull opens and the nut falls alone. The nuts are a rich dark-red mahogany, and in them lies the one objection to the tree. To some children they are poisonous, and also to grazing stock. Where these dangers can be avoided they are beautiful trees for ornamenting lawns.

Of all my country none is so truly mine as the old orchards. On almost every farm of the present day there is a deserted orchard. These trees are

Music of the Wild

Old Or-
chards worthless commercially, but at times they bear
fruit that can be used for cider at least; so their
lives are spared.   In some of these orchards the
cabin of the father or grandfather who first wres-
tled with the forest yet stands.   In many of them
the home has fallen to decay or been torn down
for firewood, but the apple trees remain even in
plowed fields and amidst growing grain.   These
trees are monuments to a deeply-rooted objection
to cutting a fruit tree, in spite of the fact that
they produce small, sour, blighted, and wormy
apples.

Almost without exception the old snake-fences
surround them, weighted with loads of growing
shrubs and vines, and on and under them home
field mice, moles, rabbits, chipmunks, lizards, birds
of low habit, night moths, and bugs and insects of
innumerable species.   The grass grows long, rank,
and so silken fine it is delightful to lie and thread
it through the fingers, and recite those exquisite
lines of Walt Whitman's,—

> "I guess it must be the flag of my disposition,
> Out of hopeful green stuff woven."

Nearly all the old orchards are on the highest
spot of a farm and near the center of the land.
These pioneers had the English plan of an estate,
with the residence in the middle, away from the
annoyance of travel and the dust of the highway.

AN OLD ORCHARD

"What plant we in this apple-tree?
Sweets for a hundred flowery springs
To load the May-wind's restless wings,
When, from the orchard row, he pours
Its fragrance through our open doors."
　　　　　　　　　—Bryant.

Songs of the Fields

But the inclination of their children seems to be to see how close to the road they can live. Indeed, many men owning several hundred acres of land covered with a half dozen valuable building sites, elevations that would insure a dry cellar, sanitary surroundings, all the breeze passing, and the seclusion that is due a family, build their homes solely with an eye to living on the road. If they are fond of surface water in their wells, which breeds typhoid fever, dust, heat, and constant trespass of travelers, no one can interfere, and the result is splendid for the birds and for me.

The farther away from the old orchard the new home is builded the surer am I of finding among the trees shy doves from river thickets, The Hymn of the Orchard brown thrashers, warblers, and bright-eyed vireos, in addition to the catbirds, bluebirds, kingbirds, robins, and screech owls that habitually home there. Also the long grass invites the larks and ground sparrows to join the chorus. And what a song it is! The rough bark of old apple trees is a table spread for larvæ seekers, and the masses of bloom a far call to insect hunters, so that from earliest spring these beautiful old orchards are the veritable choir-loft of the Lord, and from them arises one constant volume of joyful praise and thanksgiving. Even in the night the orioles nestle contentedly on their perches, and you can hear them talk about the goodness of God in their sleep.

Music of the Wild

A True Mother Fifteen feet high in the branches of one of these old apple trees a robin built her nest before leafage in the wet, cold April of 1907. There were two eggs when one morning found the cradle filled with snow, and I thought she would desert it, but later she returned. Surely brooding bird never had a more uncomfortable time. The tree had borne apples the previous year, and of course she thought it alive and expected protection from the leaves. It was quite dead, and never a sign of bloom or leaf appeared.

The weather changed abruptly each day. With no shelter whatever she sat through freezing nights, snowy days, sleet, rain, and flashes of hot sunshine. When she had four babies almost ready to leave the nest, a terrific cold rain began on Saturday morning. By afternoon it poured, and she pointed her bill skyward and gasped for breath. I fully expected that she would desert the nest and seek shelter before morning, but she remained, although drenched and half dead. That rain continued all of Sunday, pouring at times, until Monday morning. Although I watched by the hour, not once from the time it began until rifts of sunlight showed Monday morning did I see her leave her nest or feed the young, or her mate bring her a morsel of food. For an hour at a stretch, several times a day, I thought she would drown. My ladder had been erected for some time before her lo-

254

MOTHER ROBIN

When sleepy-time comes in Robin-town,
Four little heads covered with down,
Under the feathers of mother's breast,
Close against her heart are pressed.

cation, and by noon Monday I resumed a series of pictures of her nesting history. There were several dozen of them, representing every phase of her home life, the one I use here being especially individual.

Both birds attended the young alternately, with the difference that when the father fed them he removed a fæces and flew away. When the mother arrived she performed the same operation, and then, setting her breast feathers on end, slowly moved over the young, who thrust their heads against her breast, and she brooded them until the male returned. I loved to see the young move toward her and watch the sudden swell of the feathers to admit them. Several times I was tempted to record it, but thought the act was too fast for my lens. However, as I had almost everything else, I decided to try, and that morning as I detected the impulse to lift the feathers with the snuggling of the young, I snapped. The bird that disdained shelter and kept his head out when the mother moved over the nest, left it before the day was done.

Robins are true orchard birds, wonderfully friendly, and great worm consumers; in fact such fabulous numbers are fed to young robins that The Value many times over one is repaid for the few apples of a Robin and cherries they pick later. They are invaluable aids in agriculture, and every robin nest a farmer finds in his dooryard or orchard is worth five dollars to him above all the birds possibly can destroy, and the music they make, especially the song they sing in the rain, should be above price. Robins are the alarm clocks of the fields, for almost without exception they wake the morning and all birds with their glad cry, "Cheer up!"

These old orchards home many big night moths, one that reminds me of the robin. The caterpillar **An** feeds on apple leaves, and its cocoons frequently **Orchard** are spun on old trees either on a water sprout at **Moth** the base or high among the branches. The predominant color of this moth is the steel-gray of the robin, shading darker and lighter, and it has prominent markings, half-moon shaped, on its wings, almost the color of the robin's breast. It is more gaudy than the bird, however, for it also has lines of white, faint lines of black, wider ones of tan, and dark-blue circles. It is the commonest of all large moths, and is around almost every country home at night, and frequents cities as well; but because it is a creature of darkness, many people live a lifetime where it is oftenest found and never make its acquaintance.

Of all the birds that frequent orchards near **Majesty** homes, and those rarer ones that settle in my de- **in the** serted orchards, the kingbird is most appropriately **Orchard** named; for he is king, and his mate is queen, and · the apple tree they select is a palace, and the nest

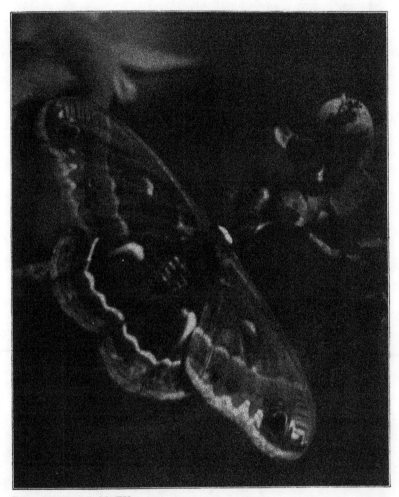

THE ORCHARD MOTH

When the sun has gone to rest,
And the moon rears her shining crest,
The night moth courts in orchard glade,
To the screech owl's wavering serenade.

is their throne-room. So ably do they defend it that never in all my life have I seen a pair conquered or their nest despoiled. The king is not such a large bird—smaller than a robin, of robingray, with a white throat and black tail having a white tip; but he is stoutly built, plump, and pugilistic, and of truly remarkable agility on wing. He has a smoky, black, rounding crest, and wings of the same color. Kingbirds give their young the worms that feed on grass blades, small flies, and moths that flutter close to the ground. They perform a variety of acrobatics on wing in search of food, poising over orchard and meadow hunting prey, and darting after it in headlong flight, with indescribable turnings and twistings of tireless wings.

This habit of food-catching in air prepares them for the battles they wage on wing, for so agile are they, so hardy, and of such unfaltering courage. that they attack anything threatening their nests. I have seen them chase crows, dusky falcons, and in one case a large hawk, in pell-mell flight across the sky, and their deft twistings enabled them to escape unharmed, while they darted savagely at heads and eyes and put their enemies completely to rout. With any bird close their own size—a mewling catbird or a jay wanting a newly-hatched nestling for desert—they make quick disposal.

Music of the Wild

There is very little art in their nests, but their eggs are beautifully decorated. The young are colored similar to their elders, the families large and so cunning as to be irresistible. No bird is more useful in an orchard, unless, indeed, it be a cuckoo, which is of great value because it eats caterpillars. In protecting an orchard from jays, hawks, and crows, such a pair of fighters saves you dozens of more gentle timid birds that carry worms and bugs by the million from fruit trees. In consideration of this you should acknowledge their royalty and offer them every encouragement to reign over your premises.

As we regard harmony, the kingbird is the least musical resident of the orchard. Tilting on a **Titled** lookout from the top of the tree in which his nest **Musicians** is placed, he uses what to me sounds like, "Ka-tic, a-tic, a-tic," for a tribal call and means of communication between pairs. His sustained song, if song it may be called, appeals to me as "Ka-tic, a-tic, querr, kerrr, kerrr!" but it is not composed of either mellow or musical tones, and is at all times inflected as if it were a continued call of defiance; so that the good folk who attribute to him a "sweet musical song, softly warbled," are the veriest romancers.

The picture here given shows a nest nearly fifteen feet high in one of these old orchards, around which I worked until the story of what I did with

262

ROYALTY IN THE ORCHARD

The apple-tree becomes a Palace,
When the Queen-bird builds her throne,
And a doughty soldier the King-bird,
As he stoutly guards his own.

these birds would sound like romance of another variety, did I not have a picture just as good as this to prove every statement I make. Not a leaf of the location was touched, but as it was a second nesting for the season, and in July, the heat was so intense that despite the shade of her chosen location the mother bird often lolled on the nest, as in this picture. The wonderful thing about it is that after a few days I placed the camera on the top of a ladder opposite the nest and near enough to secure reproductions of this size. The old birds were so convinced of my good intentions that I obtained dozens of poses as good as this, and even better, of each of them. I took their young from the nest and photographed them every day for the last four days before they left home, replaced them, and they remained even a day and a half after I had finished.

It is a truth that I can prove amply by reliable people who watched the performance from afar, that both old birds sat in the top of their 'tree and never took flight or made a sound while the young were away from the nest, and at once went on feeding them when they were replaced. Of course, I handled those young from the time they were little pin-feathered things, and they had no fear of me. If they had cried, I fancy the old ones would have been alarmed. But that birds of their universally admitted pugnacious character would permit me to handle their young, and even remove them from the nest for a half hour at a time, proves they know enough to distinguish friends from foes. It shows that even the wildest creatures can be tamed to your will by persistent kindness and unlimited patience in approaching them.

These birds are never more beautiful and interesting than when on wing, food-hunting. The waving grass of the orchard is one ground for them; the shrubs covering the fence, another. Other writers have expatiated at length on the wild rose, alder, and goldenrod that grow along these old fences; I wish to call attention to the bloom of the scarlet haw. The kingbirds taught me to notice it. I followed them to learn what insect they hunted there. I found several differing flies and gnats, and sometimes a bee was snapped up.

The scarlet haw does not bloom in crowded clusters, as does its cousin, the red haw. I have found **The Scarlet** eight blooms to a cluster, again four or five, and **Haw Choir** ten times as often six, thus establishing an average and preserving detail. Each blossom has five exquisitely cut and cupped petals, dainty stamens and pistil, and long enough stem to display the full beauty of the flower without pushing it into the others. Neither are these clusters crowded on the bush so closely as to lose their individuality, and

266

SCARLET HAW BLOOM

The bees think the cup of the scarlet haw
The finest choir-loft they ever saw.

Songs of the Fields

they bloom so late that while the leaves are yet
tender and of paler green than later in the season,
many of them are full size and dark enough in
color to form a background that emphasizes the
daintihess and purity of the blooms and makes
them the beauties of the entire haw family. The
fruit is scarlet in color and not good to eat.
The flowers will set the joy-song singing in any
appreciative heart, and their perfume calls
up a choir of half-intoxicated, nectar-loving in-
sects.

I have seen night hawks soaring late in the
evening above old orchards, and heard whip-poor-
wills cry there, but I think they only settled in Night
flight for a time, as they might in any secluded Music
in the
growth of trees. The night bird that really homes, Orchard
breeds, and lives there summer and winter is the
screech owl. It would be the funniest thing in
ornithology to see a plucked screech owl or parrot.
Small owls are such comical creatures in their
feathers, such caricatures of their great horned
relatives of the forest!

Most familiar in the orchards are the little
brown screechers, and slightly larger ones of a
cool gray, tan, brown, and black coloring. I am
very fond of them because I know so well how
happy they are, how unusually secure in the hol-
low apple tree, and how successful their hunting.
I believe they have *less* cause than many other birds

to be unhappy over anything, and so, of course, their songs are of love and contentment.

The owl has been shuddered at for a sufficient length of time. Now for a change I wish to sug- **The Owls'** gest that the people who write further history of **Serenade** him put themselves *in the bird's place and describe his song as it is sung, and not as it appeals to the interpreter's fancy.* I love to hear a screech owl screech. It means that he is having a hilarious time. His heart is bubbling over with the joy of cool, dim night life in the orchard, or throbbing with the exultation of the mating fever. He is a friendly, social bird. Every winter he comes around the cabin hunting food, and he will answer my repetition of his calls until I become uncomfortable and close the window. Every time he lifts his voice he is either locating his mate, happy enough to talk about it or pleading for a wife and home. He is the most contented bird of the orchard and almost without exception its only night singer.

A hollow apple tree is his favorite home, and from four to six the number of his children. I doubt if the anatomy of any bird contains a member more wonderful than the eye of an owl. The organ of vision is fixed in a socket so that the bird turns its head instead of its eyes, and they are surrounded by a reflector of fine, closely set feathers, while the composition of the ball is so intricate as

SCREECH ÒWL

The screech owl screeches when courting,
Because it's the best he can do,
If you couldn't court without screeching,
I ___ s ___ you'd screech too.

to merit a volume by itself. The owl can enlarge the retina, in order to see more clearly as he enters darker places. The Almighty did few things more wonderful than to evolve the eye of an owl.

I love all the music of nature, but none is dearer to the secret places of my heart than the Song of the Road. The highways are wonderful. They appear to flow between the fields, climbing hills The Song without effort, sliding into valleys, and stretching of the Road across plains farther than the eye or lens can follow. All of my roads have three well-defined wheel tracks. There are two strongly marked that every vehicle makes, and another only slightly outlined, made by those passing on the way. Tiny flowers of yellow sorrel, rank fennel, grass, dandelion, smartweed, and catnip grow to the fence corners, and these are filled with tall meadow rue, milkweed, poke berry, goldenrod, asters, thistle, saffron, teazel, and sumac sprouts. There are wild roses, alders, maple, oak, and elm shrubs, and the straggling old snake-fences are bound together and upheld by bittersweet, wild grape, honeysuckle, and moonseed.

I love the morning road, when the air is yet tinged with the dampness and mystery of night, Chants when the foliage is sharply outlined against the to the reddening sky, and every bird sings his chant as Rising Sun if he just had mastered it for a sublime offertory to a sun that never arose before. Hope is so high

18   273

in the morning. You are going to succeed where you failed yesterday. You are going to advance so far beyond anything already achieved. God is good to give to men a world full of beauty and ringing with music, and scarcely realizing it you resolve to be good as well. So you add your voice, and travel the long road in the morning with a light heart.

But after all the evening road is better, for it leads back to home and friends, and it is quite true that there is "no place like home." In the red glory of the setting sun there is the promise of light for another day; the peaceful fields appear satisfied with their growth; the birds sing vespers with a depth of harmony altogether devotional; the hermit thrush and the wood robin make your heart ache with the holy purity of their notes. And if the high hopes of the morning did not all come true, the peace of evening brings the consoling thought that perhaps you have grown enough during the day to accomplish them on the morrow; or perhaps it is best after all that success did not come. Intangible, but springing from everywhere, creeps the dark and the time of mystery; the screech owl and the whip-poor-will raise their quavering night songs, and without urging your horse lifts his tired head and breaks into a swifter trot, for night is coming, and he too is on the home road.

THE SONG OF THE ROAD

"*Afoot and light-hearted I take to the open road,*
Healthy, free, the world before me,
The long brown path before me leading wherever I choose.
Stron and content I   "

Songs of the Fields

Many volumes could be filled with the history
of old snake-fences, their inhabitants, and environ-
ment. Some of our rarest birds home in the shrub-
filled corners or swing from branches above, and
flowers of unusual beauty are found growing in
them and all along the wayside. If you do not
believe the birds are social and love the company
of human beings, compare the number of oriole
nests you can find in deep forest or open wood
with those in fields, orchards, and along roads. In
my· country I always learn after the leaves fall
that orioles in greater number than anywhere else
to be found have swung over the road above my
head in their pendant bags of hair and lint through-
out the summer.

Of all the myriad flowers that distil sweets and
call many insects to join in the song of the road
none are more beautiful than blazing star. The **Blaz-**
stems, if not bent by pushing against something **ing Star**
unyielding, grow straight toward heaven to a
height of from two to three feet where the soil is
dry, and by swampy and damper roads attain to
four, and during the season of 1907 even five.
The leaves are slender and sparsely set, alternat-
ing, and the blooms are exquisite. It is difficult to
name their shade, because it fluctuates with the
amount of moisture, exposure to sun, and the
length of time the flower has been open, but it
runs from pale violet to deep magenta-purple.

277

Music of the Wild

The bloom, sometimes an inch across, is a head of
fine petals, and reminds one of a painter's brush,
filled with exquisite color. Each little flower is
folded separately, and at maturity opens, one at
a time, around the outer rim until the whole is a
mass of shaggy, delicately colored petals. The
seed slightly. resembles larch fruit or Norwegian
pine cones, on account of being similar in shape
and covered with scales, but these are purplish-red.

One of these plants bears stamens, and another
pistils, so that they are unable to reproduce them-
selves; and were it not for the work of the bees
and butterflies in cross-fertilizing, they would
become extinct. They have enough stamens and
pollen to give a golden glow to the base of the
petals, and are of sufficient perfume to attract bees
and butterflies. Archippus, Cœnia, and Troilus do
the work necessary in carrying pollen back and
forth between plants.

The most exquisite roadside bird of which I
ever have succeeded in making a series of studies
is the goldfinch, commonly known in the country
as the "wild canary," the "lettuce" and "seed bird."
These are almost our latest migrants, wait until
July to build, and bring off but one brood in a sea-
son. The nest is a dainty affair of intricate con-
struction, and takes longer to complete than that of
any other bird I know. I have seen a pair of orioles
build their nest in three days; but the goldfinches

The Gold-Finch

MALE GOLDFINCH AND YOUNG

In a milkweed cradle, rocked by harvest winds,

Songs of the Fields

work for a week, and sometimes longer. They use quantities of plant fiber stripped from last year's dead, dry weeds, and line copiously with thistle and milkweed down. Why such deliberate and dainty architecture is not conducive to neater home-life is difficult to say; for these exquisite little birds are the filthiest housekeepers I know intimately.

Nearly all songsters—almost every bird, in fact—with its bill removes from the young the excrement, carrying and dropping it far from the nest. The goldfinches have cradles filled to overflowing, five and six young to the brood, and the elders pay no attention to this feature of parenthood, so that in a short time their nests are as white outside with a rain of droppings as they are inside with milkweed down.

The females are olive-green and yellow birds, and the males are similar in winter. In summer they don a nuptial dress, that with the pure, bubbling melody of their song must make them irresistible. They wear a black cap and sleeves, have a tail touched with black and white, and a pure lemon-yellow waistcoat. They frequent gardens, deserted orchards, and roadsides. Their song is of such bubbling spontaneity that they can not remain on a perch to sing it, but go darting in waves of flight over fields and across the road before you, sowing notes broadcast as the wind scatters the seed they love. They have a tribal call that can be imitated so they answer it readily. The male cries, "Pt'seet!" and the female answers, "Pt'see!" The continuous song that they sow on the air with an abandon approaching the bubbling notes of the bobolink, and really having more pure glee in it, to my ears syllabicates, "Put seed in it! Put seed in it!"

Possibly I thought of this because they are always putting seed into themselves. Mustard, thistle, lettuce, oyster plant, millet, and every garden vegetable and wild weed that produces a seed, in time will bear a goldfinch singing as it sways and feasts.

One of the commonest plants of the wayside, dignified and attractive in bloom, and wholly artistic in seedtime, is the milkweed. This plant is **Milk-** inseparably connected in my mind with the gold-**weed and** finch, that depends upon it for most of its nesting **Bittersweet** material, and with the monarch butterfly, the caterpillar of which feeds upon the leaves. Any plant that blankets a goldfinch family and nourishes a butterfly is an aristocrat of the first order. In touch of it grows our best-loved climber.

Because of its elegant leaves, its stout, twining stem, and brilliant and long clinging berries, the bittersweet is the very finest vine of the roadside. In winter it outshines all others, because the hulls of the yellow clusters open in four divisions and expose a bright-red berry divided sometimes into

MILKWEED

Proudly the milkweed lifts its head,
And bears its pods on high,
For it lines the dainty goldfinch nest,

Songs of the Fields

three, and again four parts, each containing a small
oblong seed. The elegant vines cover fences, trees,
climb poles, and spread over bushes all along the
road. The berries retain their brilliant color dur-
ing winter, so that on gray days they lighten the
gloom, and on white ones they contrast with a bril-
liancy that is equaled only by the scarlet heads of
the mountain ash.

Such pictures and music are the natural ac-
companiment of the old snake-fences. Whenever
I come into country abounding in them my heart The
always begins softly to sing, "Praise the Lord!" Music
of Nature
For where these old fences are replaced by wire
the farmers always make a clean sweep to the road-
side, and not the ghost of a picture or the echo
of a song is left to me. There are times when my
disappointment is so great it is difficult to avoid a
feeling of childish resentment. Sometimes I stop
my horse and attempt to preach timber conserva-
tion and the laws of attraction as applied to mois-
ture; but what has a passing woman to tell a lord
of creation busily improving his field? He is pro-
viding a few more feet of space for corn and po-
tatoes and enlarging his egotism over greater per-
sonal possessions. I notice that in making a field
most men exhibit a sense of creation. It is where
their work is made manifest. Yes, even to a
greater degree than they realize, for sometimes
when they arrogantly dismiss me and my theories

Music of the Wild

I smile as a summer storm sweeps unbroken over their field to emphasize my assertions.

Then men must seek shelter and stand helpless while a stout hickory they thought could weather such conditions alone is wrung to ribbons. The great oak left because of its value is stripped of its heart, their stock falls dead, their barns and homes ascend in smoke or their crops are beaten down with the storm or carried away with the wind, and their buildings demolished. Blest and beneficent is most of the music of nature. But when there is a storm, and the earth trembles, the heavens appear to open before our eyes; when the windharps shriek, and the big bass-drum rolls its thunder,—all other notes are hushed and forgotten. When nature presses the bass pedal and plays fortissimo we acknowledge the grandeur and irresistible power of the storm. And we see its beauty also. No other picture equals the splendor of mountains of black massing clouds, the white flare of electricity, the falling sheets of glistening water. Most of us enjoy a storm with palpitant exultation, although it is one musical performance that seldom gets an encore. But there are times when it teaches man that if he had left a few acres of forest in the middle of his land, and a border of trees around the edge deep enough for a wind-break, he would have saved his summer's labor, his home, and provided music and shade for the highway.

LIGHTNING-RIVEN OAK

" One bears a scar
Where the quick lightning scored its trunk, yet still
It feels the breath of Spring." —Br ant.

Songs of the Fields

The roads run systematically across the face of earth, singing the song of travel and commerce. Then there is a far sweeter song, sung by little streams of water, wandering as they will, in beneficent course, quenching the thirst of the earth, enhancing its beauty, and lulling us with their melody. Any one of these little streams is typical of all, but each nature-lover has his own partienlar brook that to him is most beautiful. The Song of the Limberlost

"I come from haunts of coot and hern,"

sang Tennyson of his. My Limberlost comes from the same haunts, and nothing can convince me that any running water on the face of earth is more interesting or more beautiful. I have read of the streams that flow over India's golden sands, down Italy's mountains, through England's meadows; but none of them can sing sweeter songs or have more interest to the inch than the Limberlost.

It is born in the heart of swampy wood and thicket, flows over a bed of muck or gravel, the banks are grass and flower-lined, its waters cooled and shaded by sycamore, maple, and willow. June drapes it in misty white, and November spreads a blanket of scarlet and gold. In the water fish, turtle, crab, muskrat, and water puppy disport themselves. Along the shores the sandpiper, plover, coot, bittern, heron, and crane take their pleasure and seek their food. Above it the hawk

Music of the Wild

and vulture wheel, soar, and sail in high heaven, and the kingfisher dashes in merry rattling flight between the trees, his reflection trailing after him across sunlit pools. The quail leads her chickens from the thicket to drink, and the wild ducks converse among the rushes. In it the coon carefully washes the unwary frog caught among the reeds, and the muskrat furrows deeper ripples than the stones.

What the Limberlost Knows The lambs play on the pebbly banks and drink eagerly, the cattle roll grateful eyes as they quench their thirst and stand belly-deep for hours lazily switching their tails to drive away flies. Little children come shouting to wade in the cool waters, and larger ones solemnly sit on the banks with apple-sucker rods, wrapping twine lines and bent pin hooks, supporting their families by their industry, if the gravity of their faces be token of the importance of their work. Sweethearts linger beside the stream and surprise themselves with a new wonder they just have discovered—their secret; but the Limberlost knows, and promises never to tell.

Perhaps that is what it chuckles about while slipping around stones, over fallen trees, and whispering across beds of black ooze. The Limberlost is a wonderful musician, singing the song of running water throughout its course. Singing that low, somber, sweet little song that you must get

THE SONG OF THE LIMBERLOST

When June comes down the Limberlost,
  In her bridal garments pale,
She pauses 'neath the wild plum trees,
  To weave her wedding veil.

Songs of the Fields

very close earth to hear, because the creek has such mighty responsibility it hesitates to sing loudly lest it appear to boast. All these creatures to feed and water; all these trees and plants to nourish! The creek is so happy that it can do all this, and if it runs swiftly other woods, thickets, fields, and meadows can be watered. Then the river must be reached as soon as possible, for there are factory wheels to be turned, boats to be carried, and the creek has heard that some day it is to be a part of the great ocean. When the Limberlost thinks of that its song grows a little more exultant and proud, bends are swept with swifter measure, louder notes are sung, and every bird, bee, insect, man, and child along the banks joins in the aecompaniment. All the trees rustle and whisper, shaking their branches to shower it with a baptism of gold in pollen time. The rushes and blue flags murmur together, and the creek and every sound belonging to it all combine in the song of the Limberlost.

Sometimes it slips into the thicket, as on the Bone farm; for it is impartial, and perhaps feels more at home there than in the meadows, surely The more than in cultivated fields, where the banks Whisper Song often are stripped bare, the waters grow feverish and fetid, its song is hushed, and its spirit broken. But in the thicket the birds gather very low above the surface, the branches dip into the friendly

293

Music of the Wild

floods, and it nourishes such an abundance of rank growth as men scarcely can penetrate. Then the Limberlost and the thicket hold a long conversation, to tell each other how very content and happy they are. The bed of the Limberlost in the thicket is ooze and muck, so the water falls silent while slipping over the velvet softness, with only a whisper to the birds and trees; not so loud as the song of the flags, rushes, and water hyacinths that grow on the banks. The many trees and masses of shrubs lower their tones to answer the creek, and he who would know their secret must find for himself a place on the bank and be very quiet, for in the thicket the stream will sing only the softest lullaby, just the merest whisper song.

The big turtles in the water are quiet folk. So are the sinous black snakes sunning on the bushes, and the muskrats homing along the banks. As if loth to break the dark, damp stillness with louder notes, the doves coo softly; for they, too, have a secret, the greatest of any bird in all the world. No wonder they keep together and live so lovingly, and coo and coo softly; those wild, tender, and—above all other—loving birds. One would think they would warble from the treetops and soar with the eagle, had not long years taught that modesty and tenderness are their most prominent characteristics.

For this is their secret. They are the chosen

BROODING DOVE

We think it grief, but 't is truly love,
That finds its voice in the coo of the dove.

Songs of the Fields

bird of Omnipotence. It was a dove that carried the news of release to the prisoners in the ark, and it was in the form of a dove that the Spirit of God is said to have materialized and hovered over the head of Jesus when He was baptized in the Jordan. What other bird bears honors high as these? Yet doves home in the thicket, on a few rough twigs they place their pearly, opalescent eggs, and in trembling anxiety brood and raise a pair of young that go modestly and lovingly through life, exactly the same as their parents. Nowhere else in all nature does the softly-uttered coo of a dove so harmonize with the environment as over a stream in a thicket; and no accompaniment to the murmuring voice of the Limberlost is quite so melodious as the love-song of this bird.

The thicket seems a natural home for almost every feathered creature. This because there are trees, bushes, and shrubs, with their berries, nuts, and fruits; vines and weeds bearing seed; every variety of insect and worm, and water with its supply of food, thus providing things to eat in a small space for almost every species. In spring and summer the birds have full sway; but in the fall, after the first black frost, come rugged country boys and girls and village children in search of fruit and nuts.

To some there is nothing so delicious as the black haw—white until almost ripe, then a day of mottled estate, and then such a luscious, shining black berry it has no equal; and if the birds get any they must be ahead of the boys and girls. The opossums must be before the boys at the persimmon tree, for few are left when they finish. The robins love wild grapes, and cedar birds the poke berries, and squirrels, hazelnuts.

Hazel bushes are beautiful. The leaf is something like the elm in shape, though the hazel is of finer cutting. They are nearly the same size, deeply grooved on top, and heavily veined underneath. The nuts grow from two to six in a cluster and are sheltered in a leafy, pulpy green cover with fringed edges, most artistic and, I should think, of great benefit to the decorator searching for an unhackneyed subject. There are many places where they could be used with fine effect in leather work, especially as the ripe nut is a good leather color. But the boy who reaches the hazel bushes before the squirrels gets up very early in the morning, and then only too often to find that the worms have been ahead of him; for when green the shells of hazelnut and chestnut are so very soft that beetles bore into them and deposit eggs that hatch, and the worm develops inside the shell, that hardens later. This explains why so often you crack a perfectly sound nut and find a wormy kernel.

When the Limberlost leaves the thicket and comes into the open again it does not spread, as

ON THE BANKS OF THE WABASH IN WINTER

"Announced by all the trumpets of the sky,
Arrives the snow; and, driving o'er the fields,
Seems nowhere to alight; the whited air
Hides hills and woods, the river, and the heaven."
—Emerson.

Songs of the Fields

it did on the bed of ooze; for in the firm clay soil of fields and meadows only a narrow channel is cut, and so with forces renewed by concentration it comes slipping across Bone's woods pasture. Where the Creek Mourns Through his fields, always tree-shaded, it flows, and then crosses farms whose owners I am glad I do not know; for here my creek is robbed of shelter, and left to spread ineffectually, and to evaporate in fetid, unwholesome pools. The trees are cut, and grazing stock by wading everywhere trample down the banks and fill the channel with soil; thus wantonly wasting water that in a few more years these land-owners will be digging ditches to reclaim. With broken heart it is dissipated by the sun, and a dry sob of agony is the only note raised as it painfully oozes across this land and beneath the road bridge.

Here the creek reaches deep-shaded channel once more, and bursts into song crossing Armantrout's pasture; for it is partly shaded, though many large trees on the banks are being felled. A happy song is sung on the Rayn farm, where it is sheltered by trees and a big hill. In full force it crosses the road again, slides below the railroad bridge, rounds the hill, chanting a requiem to the little city of the dead on its banks, flows through the upper corner of the old Limberlost swamp, hurries across the road once more, and so comes singing into Schaffer's meadow.

Music of the Wild

The low, open meadow covered closely with cropped velvet grass, "green pastures." where full-fed cattle lie in deep shade. Nowhere in its course to the river does the Limberlost "preen" and sing exultingly as when crossing this meadow. All the water babies travel with it, the kingfisher and the plover follow; the children play along the banks, and if it has any intuition at all, surely the creek can see gratitude in the eyes of the inhabitants of the meadow as they thrust their muzzles in the depths or stand cooling under trees. If the Limberlost loves admiration, here it receives a full share. The banks are covered with enough trees and bushes to make almost continuous shade for the waters, and a thing of beauty it goes laughing on the way to the Wabash. In fact it is so close the river here that big fish come adventuring and to spawn, and their splash is part of the music that the family living on the banks hears daily. Mr. Schaffer says that he can stand on his back porch, bait a fish, turn, and drop it into the frying-pan. This really could be done, but much as I have trespassed there I never have seen the fish on their way anywhere except to the river.

Aside from the song of the creek and the birds that follow, there comes an occasional wild duck, sometimes a loon lost in migration or slightly wounded by a hunter, and every spring and fall migrating wild geese pay a visit and add strange

302

When Spring sweeps down the river,
   With the joy of passing years,
Why should the red-bud quiver,
   And weep its pink-tinted tears?

RED BUD

Songs of the Fields

voices to the running chorus. Through Grove's meadow, adjoining, the creek is wilder and wider, and then gathering force in a last rush, with a glad song it goes hurrying to mingle with the Wabash.

The river, when swollen with the flood of spring rains, sings a sweeping, irresistible measure that carries one's thoughts by force; but this is its most monotonous production. There is little variation, and the birds are the strongest accompanists. Later, when it falls into the regular channel, it sings its characteristic song and appears so much happier and more content. I believe the river loves and does not willingly leave its bed. When a strong, muddy current it sweeps the surface from valuable fields, drowns stock and washes away fences; it works as if forced, and I like to think the task is disagreeable. At times it seems to moan and sob, while sucking around big tree trunks and washing across meadows and fields.

When it comes home again and runs in the proper channel it shouts and sings with glee the true song of the river. You can hear the water triumph as it swirls around great maple and sycamore roots, chuckle as it buffets against rocks, gurgle across shoals, and trill where it ripples over a pebbly floor. The muskrat weaves currents against its flow, the carp wallow in mucky pools, and the black bass leap in air as if too full of life to remain in their element.

Music of the Wild

The river is a house, the bed its floor, the surface its roof, and all the water-folk its residents. What a wonderful thing it would be if the water were transparent, that we might see the turtles, eels, and catfish busy with the affairs of life; bass, pickerel, and suckers maintaining the laws of supremacy, and water puppies at play! When the purple tints on its banks fade, tree-bloom baptizes it with golden pollen, and a week later showers it with snowy petals of wild plum, thorne, crab, and haw. All summer the trees drop a loosened leaf here and there, with Good Samaritan results; for these make lifeboats on which luckless wasps, bees, and worms fallen from blooming trees ride to safety and dry their drenched coats and weighted wings. Trees are the great life-saving service of the river, especially in the fall, when the water is covered with crisp, dead leaves. Many of them are needed, for the cool nights chill the insects so that they fall easily, the winds blow with unusual violence, and there are three times as many victims drowning as in summer.

Throughout the season many blooms decorate the river bank, but two stand pre-eminent: the **God's** redbud borne on a small tree, the mallow on a **Rarest** shrub. The tree flower is remarkable because it **Color** is almost the first color shown, and it breaks all over the branches like a severe attack of measles, when not the hint of a leaf is in sight. These come

KINGFISHER

"No wonder he laughs so loud,
No wonder he looks so proud,
There are great kings would give their royalty
To have one day of his felicity."
                    —Thompson.

Songs of the Fields

later in beautiful heart-shaped design, and the flowers are replaced by long, wine-red seed pods. The tiny blooms are shaped like the separate flowers of a locust spray, and of a shade our mothers spoke of as red analine. The blunt point of the bloom once was called a "pink tinted tear" by a poet, and this color flushes stronger until it becomes a deep magenta at the base, while the cup that holds it is reddish-brown.

This shade must be the rarest in all God's workshop, because He uses it so very sparingly. It is found on flower faces and in nature less often than any other. How He prizes it is proven by its appearance among the very first, at a time when we are eager for the color and perfume of spring. Our grandmothers taught us to love it on the petunia faces bordering olden flower beds. I delighted in it early on the Easter eggs my mother colored for me. It is one of the most ancient and popular of manufactured colors, chosen for reproduction, without a doubt, because nature is so miserly in its use; for only in hints and suggestions does it fleck the face of creation. First we see it on the redbud beside the river. Then as the poke berry matures it stripes the thrifty stem with gorgeous color to attract the bibulous cedar bird. In mid-summer you find hints of it on wayside blazing star, and in the fall New York asters and ironwort suggest it in their bloom.

Music of the Wild

The
Redbud's
Hour of
Glory But its time of greatest glory is in the first appearance, when anything else that may be in flower is white or faint pink and lavender, and only serves as a background for its tones of positive color. This hint of nature should be remembered well by lovers of the redbud. It is extremely choice about its setting. It refuses to tolerate color other than green, white, or modifications of its own shades. The trees are numerous along the Wabash and in the woods, so that— blooming before leafage .and almost first, and seeming to commingle with the mist and haze of early spring—they touch the horizon with a faint purple that melts into the blue of the sky and the lazy white clouds.

Then comes the time to worship the river. Not even when decorated in the gold of tree bloom is it so exquisitely lovely, so delicate to look upon. Few leaves are unfolded, and those a faint greenish-yellow; the magenta masses on the banks, the water singing loudest at high tide, the purple mists in the air, and fleecy clouds over all. Returning birds are warbling in a craze of joy at home-coming, and we look and listen with eyes and ears hungering for just this after the long days of winter.

To the accompaniment of water voices are added songs of birds on the banks, bushes, and trees, and the animals that live beside it.· The sun

310

RIVER MALLOWS

The river sings its beauty,
  While the mallow leans with grace,
And softly flushes rosy
  At sight of its lovely face.

Songs of the Fields

bird—the oriole—with breast and heart of gold, flashes above it; the cardinal, with shrill whistle, nests beside it; the catbird and jay, the robin, The Typical River Bird thrush, dove, and chat, all home along its banks, and in them nests the typical bird of the river, the kingfisher.

> "No wonder he laughs so loud,
> No wonder he looks so proud,
> There are great kings would give their royalty,
> To have one day of his felicity."

Thus sang Maurice Thompson, the sweetest musician the Wabash ever knew. Six feet the birds tunnel into a pebbly, firm embankment; on the ground deposit at least six oblong, white eggs, and the mother walls them in with regurgitated fish bones heaped around her as she broods. One family to a season is the rule, and the young remain long in the nest before they become self-supporting and add their voices to the chorus of the river.

The kingfisher is one of the birds of most ancient history, and very interesting. A large volume could be filled with tradition and story concerning it. This proves that people of all time have found it worthy of consideration. Its song is not musical according to our standards, but it is the gayest, most care-free, rollicking bird of the river, and one whose presence is almost universally

313

respected. In all my work afield I never have found a kingfisher wantonly shot, or heard of such a thing. There seems to be an understanding that they are not suitable for food, and do not interfere with other birds; so they are unmolested. They fly in dashes and perch at short intervals, making it a task for any one so disposed to harm them. The only depredation I have known them to suffer is from snakes entering their nests.

The animals that join their grunting, sniffling, and snarling with the voices of the river are the opossum, ground hog, muskrat, coon, and fox. I do not mean that all of these are river animals, but that their species home close the water, go there to quench their thirst, prey upon its denizens, and mingle their voices with its song.

Of all vegetation along the river, mallows are the typical flowers, the blooms we see most often, **The** and love best. The masses of spring color that **Queen** line the river as a rule belong quite as much to the **of River** **Flowers** fields, fences, and thickets as to the water. They are generally everywhere that a shrub remains. The mallow is a true water flower, and grows in greater beauty and blooms in a profusion unknown to its swampy relatives. The plants flourish so close to the water that half the roots are washed in the river. The succulent stems are pithy and of a golden-green color. The leaves are olive-green above and whitish underneath, slightly re-

THE SONG OF THE RIVER

The river chants a triumphal song
To the music of harping trees,
In whispers and sobs it ripples along
To the humming of the bees.

A leaping bass flings showers of spray,
A cardinal mounts on flaming wings,
And every voice of the summer day
Thrills with joy of the life it sings.

sembling maple foliage, but they are more artistically cut.

The buds are incased in a big, loose, heavily veined covering that opens to permit their exit, and this cover is set in a fringed cup, adding an artistic touch. The rosy, delicate, pink bloom emerges in a crumpled, folded state, and slowly opens and stretches to a smooth trumpet-shaped flower, as the wings of a moth expand and grow even; and it appears in late July and August, when it has a solid green background to emphasize its beauty and scarcely a rival to attract attention from it. There are five petals of the bloom, maroon at the base, abruptly shading to delicate pink at the edges, and strongly veined with maroon color on the outside. The flowers measure from four to six inches across and closely resemble pink hollyhocks. At the base the stamens and pistils combine in a tube that spreads in a pollen-covered tip and attracts bees and all sweet-lovers to the plant. When the petals fall, the case that opened for their exit closes again, and the seeds ripen inside. From pods that I gathered beside the river I have two mallow plants growing at my well curb. They were kept during winter and planted in early spring. Mallows bear cultivation easily in sufficiently damp places, but they can not have too much water.

The river with its accompanying voices forms

Music of the Wild

a characteristic part of the Song of the Fields;
a pure, liquid note tinged with serene and tranquil
River melody sung from a perfect setting, and perhaps
Voices draws a larger audience than any other music of
the open. Because the fields are the scene of man's
greatest activity, the voice of toiling humanity is
their dominant note.

The roar of great cities, the screaming of lake,
river, and railroad traffic, and the busy hum of
workers in the fields combine in the song of life.
But bare and unadorned existence is an ugly, sor-
did thing, so some men have kept all the beauty
they could. That part of the original gift of the
Lord to the children of men that they themselves
have preserved furnishes every picture it rests our
weary eyes to see and every note our tired ears
care most to hear—the divine and unceasing Song
of the Fields.

PART III

Music of the Marsh

"Angles of water-fowl winnowed the purple sky,
Clanging their trumpet notes
As if from brazen throats,
And seeming to fan the star-dust with their wings."
                                                    —Thompson.

GOD'S FLOWER GARDEN

Come with me and you shall know
The garden where God's flowers grow.
Come with me and you shall hear
His waters whisper songs of cheer.

The Music of the Marsh

"**P**AT O'ROURKE! Pat O'Rourke! Pat O'Rourke!" rolls Father Bullfrog's basso profundo.

"Got drunk! Got drunk! Got drunk!" echoes Mother Bullfrog's contralto, responsive.

"Keel 'im! Keel 'im! Keel 'im!" pipes the youngster's shrill treble.

Thus the frogs sing the opening chorus. Through earth's long winter sleep the marsh lies the barest and dreariest of places. With the first black frost all its tender, succulent water plants and vines droop their graceful heads and become masses of decaying vegetation. Stripped of June's riot of foliage and bloom, the bushes stand bare and scraggy. The trees reach heavenward stark branches, like bony fingers, as if imploring the powers of nature to come quickly and reclothe

The Prelude

323

Music of the Wild

them in their coats of living green. Somber and almost deserted the marsh lies, while above it towers the woodpecker's drum, a monument to loneliness.

Then comes Jack Frost, waving his magician's wand and transforming the gray old marsh to a scene of splendor. Not a tree, bush or log does he miss when he spreads his white robe and scatters his jewels; and his lace-webbed work on fine vines and weeds is most beautiful of all. Betimes a cardinal flashes like a tongue of flame across the white sheen, powdering his gay plumage with crystals as he searches for seeds or rocks on a twig and sings to the world of "Good cheer!" Again, a song sparrow bravely pipes in the face of ice and snow, a falcon cries or a hawk screams. Small gray titmice chatter socially as they search for seed, and crows, appearing their biggest and blackest in this white setting, keep watchful eyes for the sleeping quarters of all smaller birds.

From hollow trees the squirrels loudly bark. There are long irregular trails across the snow where the furred people go hunting, and down to the water to drink, and trampled places where the cotton-tails dance in the moonlight. And always, with darkness, from big hollow sycamores slip the only feathered singers of winter nights—the owls —with faces to fear, soundless wings, and dreadful claws, to prey on other musicians.

THE RESURRECTION

"I heard a whisper sweet and keen
Flow through the fringe of rushes green,
The water saying some light thing,
The rushes gayly answering."
                              —Thompson.

The Music of the Marsh

At last the sun creeps nearer and smiles' ardently, and the heart·of the pregnant marsh grows warm. The winds come sweeping with wailing notes and carry away earth's leafy covering: the rains pour, and vegetation springs to meet them. As soon as silky catkins hang from the willows and frogs sing their first chorus, only a few days are required to transform the bare old earth into summer fairyland. Graceful, gayly-colored plants and flowers lift their heads everywhere. Like magic, water grasses, cattails, flags, ferns, and delicate lacy, twining vines spring up to cover the black muck, while moss and air plants trail overhead. Every stump and log has a bright velvet dress, and crimpled lichen faces renew their unending shades of gray and green.

Pond lily pads reach the surface and spread over acres of water, their covering of golden green with tints of purple underneath furnishing choir-lofts for the frogs, sun parlors for tiny turtles, and good hunting grounds for small, wire-legged sanderlings. Above them yellow lilies thrust leaves of ranker growth, and these in turn are crowned with the heart-shaped foliage of water hyacinth. Then come the sweet marsh grasses, blue flags, and foxfire, topped with waving cattails and bulrushes, and high above all the graceful wild rice waves its feathery plumes.

The marsh flowers form masses of positive col-

327

oring. Pearl white and pearl fine are the lustrous blooms of the arrowhead. White pond lilies lift faces of snow to the morning and resemble star reflections at night, while the yellow are the purest gold of nature's alchemy. Water hyacinths and blue flags flash back the azure of the sky above them, and clumps of foxfire blaze like flaming torches.

On the tops of the highest mountains can be found evidence that they once were submerged, and so I imagine that as the water receded, in the beginning, the whole earth was one great marsh. When the waters evaporated or were pushed back by eruptions, the highest places were left bare, the next highest grew forests, the lower remain marsh, and the lowest lakes and seas.

The road to the marsh is not so difficult to find as that to the forest. Men learn that it is easier **The** to fell and burn trees than to control water in **Road to** depth and quantity. The marsh road probably **the Marsh** will be either deep sand or corduroy laid in a bed of muck; a mere path to the object of your goal, but on either side of it lies the garden of the Lord. Acres upon acres of the most brilliant color waving above man-height, interlaced by delicate vines and watered with fountains springing naturally from the wet bosom of earth and flowing away in tiny streams so narrow they are soon lost beneath the flowers closing over them, and so cold they

THE ROAD TO THE MARSH

One misty, dreary August morning,
*When the **sunshine** left without giving warning.*

The Music of the Marsh

seem as if ice-chilled, each bank fringed with water cress.

The masses of flowers are made up of golden-rod, aster, ironweed, Joe Pye-weed, milkweed, swamp laurel, cardinal flower, turtlehead, and daisies peeping wherever they can reach the light. There are cone flowers, swamp sunflowers, everything you know, and others the books fail to name, among the vines and mosses especially; and all of abnormal growth from the rich muck, warmth, and the abundance of water.

Although it is not so easy to attack the swamp as the forest, on all sides man is pressing close. Big ditches are being dredged, leading from the marshes lying highest on the face of earth to lower bodies of running water, so that the marsh level is reduced by several feet, giving an unbelievable amount of space that soon dries for cultivation. I know of homes being built so close the marsh that water rises in your footsteps between rows of cultivated vegetables. Everywhere the marsh is driven back, and as it recedes men hurry in with garden truck first, and grain later.

The character of wild growth changes as moisture is removed. Mullein and thistle take the place of flowers of damper habit. Because they are so tall, so delicate, and of such clear, exquisite blue, marsh lilies (*Camassia fraseri*) are conspicuous above any. They grow where it is slightly high

331

Music of the Wild

and sandy, but close the water, and spring from a deeply-rooted bulb. The leaves are like those of a tuberose, and from a tall, slender stem grow single flowers forming a cluster that slightly resembles hyacinths. They are loaded with pollen, and the wild honey-bee and all species of bumblebees, in fact, ants, flies, and sweet-lovers of every family, feast upon them. They are one of the rarest and most beautiful blues of nature, and the music around them is unceasing.

The Bumble-bee Choir

From the top of an elevation from which the sweet marsh grass had been shorn I looked down to a cultivated strip bordering a marsh, last August. I could see blades of corn waving, and distinguish a solid mass of peculiar blue-green. Making my way through the intervening swamp, and climbing a fence buried in bloom, I came to the queerest effort at cultivation I ever had seen. From a layer of soil so thin that it would not bear my weight without quivering beneath me the flowers had been mowed, and with such cultivation as could be given with a hoe were growing the finest cucumbers and cabbage imaginable. The picture I made there illustrates the character of the soil and proves how closely men are pressing the marsh, as no words of mine can.

It was Thoreau who, in writing of the destruction of the forests, exclaimed, "Thank Heaven, they can not cut down the clouds!" Aye, but they

MARSH LILIES

"Every tongue of Nature sings;
The air is palpitant with wings."
                    —*Thompson.*

The Music of the Marsh

can! That is a miserable fact, and soon it will become our discomfort and loss. Clouds are beds of vapor arising from damp places and floating Cutting Down the Clouds in air until they meet other vapor masses, that mingle with them, and the weight becomes so great the whole falls in drops of rain. If men in their greed cut forests that preserve and distil moisture, clear fields, take the shelter of trees from creeks and rivers until they evaporate, and drain the water from swamps so that they can be cleared and cultivated,—they *prevent vapor from rising;* and if it does not rise it can not fall. Pity of pities it is; but man can change and is changing the forces of nature. I never told a sadder truth, but it is truth that man can "cut down the clouds." In utter disregard or ignorance of what he will do to himself, his children, and his country he persists in doing it wherever he can see a few cents in the sacrifice.

And of all the dreary, desolate places for a home these little cabins perched on a small elevation at the edge of a marsh are the worst, especially in the mists of morning and evening. I can see the artistic possibilities of the gray cabin, the heavy mists, the drenched grasses, the straggling, vine-covered old fences, and the vapor-shrouded trees and swamp. It is all most beautiful, but so desolate. As a setting for a funeral it is appropriate, but as a home it appeals to me as insupportable. Home means solid foundations, light, pure air, congenial surroundings; and while the marsh is the most beautiful place in the whole world in summer; in early spring, late fall, and winter it is bare and cheerless. In recompense for this, summer outdoes herself in a babel of music, masses of glowing flower color, delicate mosses too fragile to touch, and swaying vines festooned everywhere they can find something to which to cling.

One lovely swamp vine that I never have seen used in decoration or conventionalized or in fact **Ground Nut** reproduced anywhere outside botanies, is the ground nut. Unfortunately for my study, the only perfect vine I ever have found grew on that thing I most detest, disfiguring the face of nature—a wire fence. This fence crossed a tract so swampy, rails soon decayed, and wire was substituted. The location was on the banks of the Elkhart River, in a very marshy country.

The vine springs from a pear-shaped tuber that botanists pronounce edible. The leaves grow along a stem, five to a group. The ground nut bloom clusters slightly resemble wistaria, but in beauty and exquisite perfume far exceed its loveliest flowers. The bean-shaped blossoms are essentially so wild, so of the swamps. They grow in a short tassel, are of rich brown and maroon color, and as clusters are turned in the light a changeable shade of lilac shows strongly; and added to

336

A MARSH GARDEN

They cut God's brightest flowers away,
   Dropping each swaying, graceful head,
And used the earth whereon they grew
   To make a cabbage bed.

The Music of the Marsh

that, the entire surface of the bloom is of texture velvet-fine. A short distance away the blooms smell like the sweetest of English violets; closer, a touch of pungency that is pure wildness can be discerned.

Held to light the flower presents lilac shades on the outer surfaces, maroon in the middle distances, and rich, velvety brown in the depths. All the plant requires is fertile, damp soil to make a vigorous growth; so it is easily domesticated. For downright grace and richness of coloring it surpasses any cultivated vine of which I can think at this time, and being edible, there would be no danger in transplanting it.

Another delicious plant of the marshes is water cress. Wherever there are streams fed by springs and cold enough to harbor trout, there pungent water cress grows. The leaves and stems of this plant at its prime make one of the most appetizing and healthful salads known. It grows from six to ten inches in height, with brownish, dark-green leaves in early spring, gradually becoming lighter as summer advances. The leaves are round and form compound clusters of from three to nine. The tiny white flower is insignificant.

Its scientific term is *Nasturtium officinale*, derived from the Latin *nasus*, meaning nose, and *tortus*, twisted; the name originating from the fact that pungent odors of the plant sting and

Music of the Wild

twist sensitive organs. So extremely thrifty is this water member of the nasturtium family along creeks and cold running water that I know large streams that are literally choked with cress, running through miles of unbroken marsh. The music is threefold. There is water ten inches deep whispering and gurgling around the stems, bees visit the blossoms, and the human voice rings loudly and clearly when a bed is discovered in early spring; for this is just the tonic needed to thin sluggish winter blood. The biting tang is craved by the system, and a shout of joy greets the discovery; so it, too, has a place in this music-book.

There is more human as well as bird and insect music every time a lover of nature on his way to **Silky** the marsh finds a bed of *Cornus amomum* in **Cornel** bloom. It grows from two to six feet high, and leaves densely before it flowers; there is an especial cluster around the blooms. These heads are made from masses of fine white flowers, each having four wide-open petals, an exaggerated set of stamens, and long pistil, so that the pollen, when ripe and dusty, gives a golden tinge to the entire white cluster.

Quantities of this pollen must be used by tame bees, or else there is a worldful, having the same snappy, tart wild tang; for the bees of country hives make honey that has precisely this flavor. In the fall each flower cluster is represented by

340

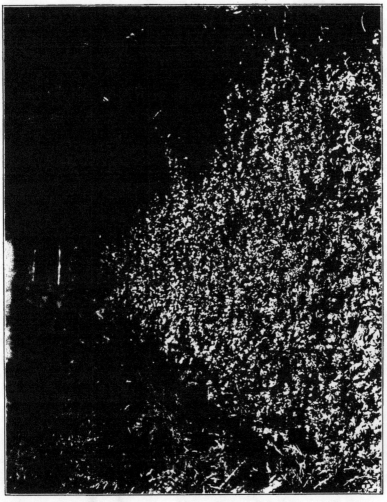

THE NOSE TWISTER

"Vines are the curtains,
Blossoms the floor;
Voices of waters
Sing evermore."
—Taylor.

The Music of the Marsh

a bunch of hard berries, at first green, later almost white, and not good to eat.

In early June on any thorn or willow growing along the road to the marsh a short search will reveal a treasure that I do not understand why The Moth of the Marsh poets fail to sing. You find a dangling, oblong cocoon, hanging from a twig by a bit of spinning. The outside appears as if it were coated with lime and then wrapped in leaves, whose veining shows with remarkable clearness. All the long winter, during the cold rains, snows, ice, and winds, it hangs and is buffeted; but by late May or early June a wet spot develops on the top. Soon a struggling big night moth climbs out and clings with its feet to the under side of a limb.

There the crumpled wet wings straighten, expand, and develop a sweep of from six to six and a half inches—larger than a wren—and take on an indescribable richness of color. Almost every shade from lightest tan to dark-brown makes up a complicated series of linings and veinings, that are brighter in color on the upper side and touched with pink. Each wing has a transparent eye-spot like isinglass, so that print can be read through it, and the body and feet are covered with long, fine, velvety down.

The moths fly the first night after they emerge; mate, deposit their eggs, and soon die. The caterpillar that hatches, eats thorn or willow leaves,

Music of the Wild

grows for five or six weeks, then spins a cocoon
around itself, and lies dormant during the winter,
developing another big moth that will flit above
the marshes, fields, and towns the coming June,
and awake a joy song in the heart of every one
who sees it.

Typical marsh begins with cultivated land run-
ning down to a stretch of wild growth that shades
off into masses of water grasses, cattails, and bul-
rushes.   These in turn are edged by true water
flowers, hyacinths, blue flags, arrowhead lilies, then
the water; and that covered for acres with yellow
lilies near the shore, farther out the spreading
leaves and masses of white flowers blanketing as
much more of the surface, and next clear, deep
water in which you can row and fish.

At first, in crossing the waters of a marsh, the
eye is almost blinded and the senses stunned by
the glory of the masses of colors, and as you be-
come accustomed to fairyland a roll of swelling,
throbbing sound fills the ears.

Then, ho, for the music of the marsh! It be-
gins with the frogs. When the first faint breath
The of catkin pollen tinges the wind, morning and
Chorus of evening vesper is caroled by a babel of voices and
the Frogs a pæan of praise greets every passing shower.
The moment the sun shows his face, orange-bellied
tree-toads with backs like an unusually brilliant li-
chen plaster themselves to limbs from which it is

344

THE MOTH OF THE MARSH

Her empty house beside her dangles,
While her jeweled wings she tries;
Waiting a mate in perfumed tangles,
Where the shining marsh moth flies.

The Music of the Marsh

almost impossible to distinguish them, and in solo,
duet, and full chorus set up a never-ending peti-
tion for more rain. Bullfrogs drum until one
wonders what would be the size of their bodies
were they in proportion with their vocal powers.

But it is only for a few days that the frogs
are allowed to monopolize the music, for when the
green hyla pipes and the bullfrog drums, the en-
tire aquatic orchestra and the full chorus make
haste to join them. Nowhere else in nature do
scales, fur, feathers, and gauzy-winged things
meet in such commonalty. Here black bass, musk-
rat, and blue heron seek their food in the same
water.

Marsh music is unceasing, and it is all so good.
As you guide your boat between the rushes and
glide softly over the lily pads, sweet as Æolian **Marsh**
harps is the music of the wind sobbing among the **Music**
branches, the rushes rustling with each passing
breeze, the grasses whispering together, and the
softly lapping water. You hear crickets singing
as cheerily as beneath the hearthstone; grasshop-
pers voicing constant praise of the sweet marsh
growth; honey-ladened wild bees droning over the
pollen, and swaying snakefeeders singing on the
rushes.

O, how the snakefeeders swing and sing, and
how beautiful they are! There are many mem-
bers in the family, all of bright color; a trim head,

347

Music of the Wild

big eyes, a slender, long body, dainty legs, and
four wings set in pairs on each side, with a strong
costa or rib along the front edge, the remainder
the transparent isinglass of the locust. They have
a pair of sharp grinders in the mouth, and feed on
small insects among the rushes. As every living
creature has equal rights to life with all others,
the tragedy is quite as great when a dragon fly
pounces upon a water spider and tears off its legs
and eats the body as when a hawk sweeps down
upon a partridge and carries it away.

Dragon flies are the typical insects of the
marsh, and of beauty surpassing all others. Not
only are their bodies brightly colored, but their
wings glitter as diamonds in the light. They have
curving, jointed antennæ, and grow to a wing-
spread of four inches in some larger species, so
that they attack prey the size of cabbage butter-
flies. They deposit their eggs in water, and their
young are aquatic until time to take wing; when
they crawl on the rushes, burst their covering,
and emerge damp and crumpled, like night moths.
Soon, however, their wings expand and harden,
and they begin to flash their glancing colors over
the marshes and sing their song on the thwarts of
your boat; yes, even on the brim of your hat. They
stray far inland, and often when on the road to
the marsh you can see them hunting through beds
of rank bergamot and cone flower, ruthlessly de-

DRAGON FLY

"Where the dusky turtle lies basking on the gravel
Of the sunny sand-bar in the middle tide,
And the ghostly dragon fly pauses in his travel
To rest like a blossom where the water lily died."
                                        —Riley.

The Music of the Marsh

stroying every small sweet-hunter to be found; so
that they become veritable dragons, and their name
applies to them rarely well.

These same beds of bergamot deserve a pass-
ing mention. In botanies they are located on
higher ground, but no dry place ever bred them Marsh
in such profusion as the margin of some swamps Bergamot
I know. The illustration here given was made of
flowers that grew in a damp approach to a marsh,
and the bergamot was so thrifty it waved grace-
ful heads high above me in the summer of 1907,
and also over yellow cone flowers, that in dry lo-
cations are usually taller. This bed of bergamot
grew from six to eight feet in height and spread
along my path for the greater part of a quarter
of a mile in just such profusion as is shown in this
study. I doubt if the plant ever surpassed the
growth here shown. The hairy stems grew straight
and slender, the sharply pointed leaves were rough,
having a whitish cast, and the flowers were a large
head, from which sprang many small trumpet-
shaped blooms, with a prominent upper lip grow-
ing fine hairs. The center stamens and pistil were
of stronger color. The blooms were a pale ma-
genta-purple, at times almost pure lavender, and
you knew you were close the heart of nature when
you smelled them. Their perfume struck the nos-
trils as the tang of a wild apple excites the palate.
It brought the savage to the surface and made one

Music of the Wild

cry with Walt Whitman, "I think I could turn me and live with the animals."

There is music in the voices of the furred people. It may sound like sniffling, grunting, and **Animal** growling to us, but that is because we fail in our **Talk** translations. They are searching for food, building their homes, raising their babies, loving and caring for their mates just as do human folk, and when undisturbed all their notes are of love and tenderness.

There is music in the water. Can you name a sweeter note than the splash of the black bass so full of abundant life it can not keep beneath the surface? And how fond it is of making this music everywhere except in the immediate vicinity of your boat! You may drag up your muck and moss-ladened anchor until your back aches, and row in pursuit until your hands blister; but always you hear the music of the splash and see the widening circles of waves from a leaping bass just a short distance away.

Where deep water meets those reeds and rushes that grow beneath the surface, the variety fishermen **Water** call "bass-weeds," the children of nature are close **Voices** together, and creatures of land and water habit find themselves in touch. Such shores are beautiful, and in great marshes stretch away endlessly. Living creatures are so numerous you need not linger to study their music; it travels with you.

MARSH BERGAMOT

"Were I in churchless solitudes remaining,
Far from all voice of teachers and divines,
My soul would find, in flowers of God's ordaining,
Priests, sermons, shrines!" —Smith.

The Music of the Marsh

You can hear what the lark tells the cardinal, the cardinal tells the heron, the heron tells the duck, the duck tells the turtle, the turtle tells the muskrat, the muskrat tells the bass, the bass tells the water puppy, and the water puppy tells the eel, all along your way. The story is musical because it is recitative of freedom, living, and loving.

But of all nature's minstrelsy the palm always must be awarded the birds. The fact that the music of the marsh is distinctive to the location, The Bird only makes it dearer to those so in sympathy with Chorus it as to interpret aright. Long before the marsh is ready to receive them its feathered denizens are hovering over it, filling the air with exquisite song while they wait the laying of the foundation on which to begin the superstructure of their homes. Marsh wrens intersperse their love-making with scolding chatter because the rushes grow so slowly. While they wait, red-winged blackbirds, true children of the marsh, rock on the flags and swell their throats with notes so liquid and golden that in all birdland the most exquisite singer can produce but a faint breath of harmony above their "O-ka-lee!" and "Con-quer-eee!"

Counting out the pervasive, black-coated crow, a permanent resident, the killdeer is the first musician to reach the marsh. In early seasons he arrives in March; under any conditions he is sure in April. When flocks of these birds circle against the sun, high above you their breasts gleam silver-like, and they fling through space their lovable "Kill-deer, kill-deer!" cry until you recognize in them one of the attractions that draws you there. Over desk and counter all the long winter you have hungered for their exquisite notes. Now they are a treat for your ears, and your eyes follow the graceful gleaming figures across the sky with admiration and interest you never before realized you had felt in them.

Enough of the instinct of the plover family clings to the killdeer to induce us to believe it is **Killdeer** a true marsh bird, for it lands there on arrival and **Notes** hunts food until it is plentiful everywhere. But when nesting-time comes it is quite as likely to seek upland and prairie as to remain around the marsh. Two peculiarities of a brooding killdeer are always worth mentioning. Since the nest is a mere hollow of earth, with only a few clods and chips drawn together, the eggs are so colored as to be indistinguishable from their surroundings, and so sharply pointed that the severest winds only circle them on their bases, but do not roll them away. As a further preventive of this the mothers always place them with the four sharp points nosing each other in the nest.

Also, the killdeer is so fanatically devoted to its young that its tones are plaintive with anxiety. A great difference can be distinguished be-

SILKY CORNEL

"There is some one must hear the tune,
And feel the thrilling words,
As flowers feel in early June,
The wings of humming-birds."
—Thompson.

tween the notes of the male away pleasuring and those of the brooding mother. Early in incubation she deserts her nest as readily as any other bird; near its close, when she feels against her breast the workings of small feet and wings quickening into life, when to her ears come the first faint calls of her shell-incased babies, the music of Elysium has touched her heart, she becomes possessed with the spirit of martyrdom, ready to die at her post. If she sees your approach in time to dart a rod from her nest, by feigning a broken wing she almost invariably can tole you from her location. If you take her unaware she stands astride her eggs, valiantly pecking at your hand, and frequently suffering your touch like a brooding domestic bird.

Who that has seen a killdeer nestling can blame her? In all bird-babyland there is nothing more cunning to see or more appealing to hear. They have a tiny, wedge-shaped body little over an inch in length; a small, sharp beak for probing; a cap of speckled pepper and salt, with a black band and a white visor; a broad collar, snowy white, with a black tie; a white vest shading to delicate salmon in the under parts; a coat and upper sleeves to match the cap crown, with elbow bands of black and lower sleeves of white, and the legs bare well above the second joint for wading. This is as it should be; for, think what a pity to soil so elegant a suit

Music of the Wild

merely to appease the appetite! And how these tiny legs fly! In fright or excitement they flash across the sand and stones with such rapidity that you can not distinguish their motion, and the babies appear like small airships.

In all marsh music there is no more plaintive and wholly sweet tone than their faltering, pleading baby notes in rendering the tribal call of the family. They pipe it out as if uncertain about its being right, but perfectly confident that it will bring protection, provided they make it sufficiently pathetic. There never should be any wonder that these mothers so valiantly risk their lives for their babies.

The wonder should be if they did not; and when we stop to think of it we realize that it is for these things we love them. To know the killdeer is to delight in its music and respect its character. Excepting the upland species, that also like marshy places, the remainder of the members of the plover family are more constant to the marsh, taking pleasure trips, nesting and raising their babies, and their notes are among the most attractive of its music. They have three distinctive utterances commouly heard.

The common plover note is a clear, penetrating whistle, long-drawn, mellow, resonant—beautiful music. Their mating cry, very seldom heard except between a pair busy with household affairs

Infant Pipings (margin note)

362

WILD RICE

"Ho, for the marshes, green with spring,
Where the bitterns croak and the plovers pipe,
Where the gaunt old heron spreads his wing,
Above the haunt of rail and snipe."
—Thompson.

The Music of the Marsh

of gravest importance, is a loud, mournful wail, resembling the sobbing of a November wind among the pines. Like the killdeer's note, it is so tinged with parental concern that, being heard by hunting parties coming in at night, it causes an involuntary shudder. When disturbed in brooding, the female screams lustily, much like a half dozen other marsh birds; and her mate answers from afar with a strident insistence that might be interpreted as an effort to encourage her to remain on her nest. He thrashes among the grass and rushes, and makes a big demonstration, but it ends at that, for he keeps his distance.

The Whistling Plover

When brooding is over and flocks of plover are caring for and pleasuring with their young, they have a grand concert that is delightful and alluring. They congregate around the mouth of some small creek that empties into the marsh, skimming low over the water and hunting food close the roots of the marsh weeds and flowers. This is real plover music. Then the peeping and cheeping of the young and the chatter and chirp of the old ones resemble in volume the vocalizing of ducks. Their notes grow clearer and sweeter, more nearly like those of a songbird.

They are small, plump-breasted, friendly bodies, that in dry weather go tilting over rotten logs, and with sharp, dainty bills probe the moss for worms. Four in a row they line up and watch

365

Music of the Wild

a boat drift by close enough to photograph them. The coming of a storm develops their true plover nature. Then they are a sight to see, and rare music to hear. Skimming along close to the surface of the water, darting through reeds and rushes, wheeling, dipping, alert, full of life and grace, they become for the time different birds from their dry weather selves. They seem exalted, glorying in the tumult of the elements, and as they sail with the storm or wheel and beat against the face of it,—O, what music! Clear, sweet, pure of tone, scarce a note in the marsh can surpass it.

Good hunting to his liking adds the rattle of the kingfisher to the marsh chorus early in May. His coat is as vivid a spot in air as the sweet flag and water hyacinth below him. Among these somber-robed marsh musicians his bright color is a delight to the eye; his rollicking call a series of jolly notes good to hear. They may not embody so much melody, but there is nothing sneaking about them. They give fair notice of his coming and intentions.

Does the word "sneak" call to mind the crow? He belongs to the marsh choir—he is a part of its daily life, his notes come with greater frequency and intrusion than those of any other bird. He is constantly slipping everywhere and peering into nests, to the sorrow of many smaller musicians; for he is dangerous near eggs and young.

The sweetest sound marsh music sends,
To the ears of its listening lover,
Is a long-drawn note, mellow and clear,
The voice of the whistling plover.

The Music of the Marsh

"Caw, caw, caw, cawk," he cries from every tree-top and stump.

When the tall marsh grasses and the blue flags wave as with the sinuous passage of a large snake, and a low, steady, prolonged "Um-um-um-um" The King Rail Performs comes booming across the water, know that you are poaching on the preserves of a king rail, and that the male bird is going into an impromptu convulsion in the hope of luring you from his nest. If you follow and search for him you may catch a glimpse of an elegant, bright brown water bird darting between the stems of the grasses among which he feeds.

But if you remain in your first location and search until you find his home, you will see that nature seldom has been more generous with the The Cradle of Royalty treats she has in store for her lovers. The nest, eggs, and home life of the king rail are beautiful things, and should be known by every friend of the marsh. Search for a hummock only a few inches above the water, where the dead, dry, straw-colored grass blades of last year are trampled into a large, flat, bowl-shaped nest. It is slightly lined with finer grasses and a few feathers of a rich dark-brown color, twice narrowly banded with white, plucked from the breast of the mother near the butt of the wing. Here are cradled as many as twelve whitish eggs, sparsely sprinkled with small reddish spots, and splotched with larger markings of pale lavender that have the effect of being dabbled on with a brush and seen through an oily veiling. Then the tops of the flags and young grasses are caught and deftly woven into a cool green arch above the rich straw-colored bed that holds these rarely beautiful eggs, making a picture that must be seen to be appreciated fully.

Some experience will be required in detecting a location, so slightly does the roofing of the nest affect the general appearance of the marsh. Careful searching will reveal the "run-a-way," usually at the northeast, through which the slender-bodied mother slips to feed and rest.

If you have the luck to find a nest after a few days of brooding so has burned the mother heart A Queen that she will remain, you will become ac-Mother quainted with a lovely, graceful bird, whose poise, dignity, and extreme courage will compel your admiration and make you wish her voice were sweetest music as would seem befitting her splendid presence. Her long, dark beak is finely cut and curved. Her eyes are so wise, and filled with steady, tender devotion. Her coloring is a rich brown, quite dark on the top of the head, lighter in a streak running from the base of the beak above the eye and on the throat, and lining across the back of the wings in varied marking of brown, black, and white with beautiful V-shaped effects.

If you touch her or go too close she utters a

A QUEEN MOTHER   *Where the Queen of all the marsh birds,*
Royal in her emerald nest,
Rules as in Venetian palace,
On the water's shimmering breast.

The Music of the Marsh

rasping "Gyck, gyck," but she does not desert her
nest and eggs. True men admire motherhood.
No spot in their hearts is so tender as the place
for wife and child. No sight is so appealing as
that of a mother shielding her baby. These birds
are mothers also, with true, maternal instinct.
When you look into the brave eyes of this feath-
ered mother, one of nature's shyest, wildest crea-
tures, that fears you as death, yet steadily remains
on her nest for the sake of the mites she is pro-
tecting,—take off your hat to one of the finest ex-
hibitions of courage you ever will be permitted
to see.

While you are becoming acquainted with her,
away in the marsh the grasses bend as before a
strong wind with the frantic rushes of her agon- Character-
ized mate, who answers her cry with a sharper *istic* Music
"Gyek, gyck," and rumbles his groaning "Um-
um-um-um," making the nearest approach to the
boom of a bittern of any other marsh bird. It
may not be the most pleasing music, but coming
from strong characters with brave hearts, it com-
pels warm sympathy always.

The king rail is a wader with slender bare legs
and feet, neither webbed nor lobed, but having
long, slim toes with sharp nails. A marsh adja-
cent to a corn field is his chosen location. His
favorite diet is seed rich in starches, from the weeds
and grasses, that make him a plump, dainty dish

Music of the Wild

for the epicure by fall, when he is fair game in season.

To look at the cattails and swamp grasses growing five and six feet tall, and the graceful heads of wild rice like feather dusters sweeping the sky and scattering seeds over the water, one would think the food on which the rail fattens would be lost; but when the Almighty works out a design in nature there are no missing parts, and the mind of man must study deeply to comprehend His plans and providences. Wherever the wild rice and seed grass grow for the food of marsh birds, beneath you will find that the Lord has spread a table of stout, overlapping lily pads, upon which He scatters the seed with the winds, and the birds dine royally. They are very fond of wild rice, and some birds eat the seed of the yellow pond lily that ripens in peculiar cone-shaped heads.

When your boat slips through the mists of earliest morning the first note you will hear is the **The** long, shrill "Kuw, kuw, kuw!" of the cinereous **Herald** coot. At its best the performance of the herald **of Dawn** of dawn is only slightly touched with melody, but it is a distinctive note that you would miss if you did not hear; for it is a part of that first eager, throbbing joy that grips your throat and thrills your heart over your initial day of freedom for the season.

You will recognize the tribal call, a short, hard

374

THE MARSH BROOK

A sweet low song the marsh brook sings
As it glides by Joe-Pye-Weed and thistle.
Accompanied by bees and crisp insect wings,
And the notes of the plover's gay whistle.

The Music of the Marsh

"Pitts, pitts!" as one you frequently have heard around your boat, even if you never have seen the bird. Like all marsh residents in excitement or anger, the coot screams—a deep, guttural cry, most unpleasant, and music that can be avoided easily; for he will not perform it unless you trample on his rights and provoke him.

The coot appears to be the connecting link between the wading and the swimming birds. It is a queer compound, having the compact body of the grain-eater, the long, bare legs of the wader, and the lobed feet of a swimmer. It is a true marsh bird, avoiding lakes and running water, breeding and pleasuring among the reeds and rushes, and swimming in the open pools. It is almost as expert a diver as the grebe, but the lobed feet that make it such a splendid swimmer are slightly awkward on land; and though a fairly good runner, it is not nearly so agile as the rail.

Perhaps this watchman, who for centuries has announced to the marsh the first red peep of coming day, has tinged his coat by long contact with the black muck and water. Aside from the mourning of the crow, and the brighter black lit by iridescent gleams of the blackbird, the coot is the most somber-robed musician of the marsh. He wears a suit of dark steel-gray, shading to black on the wings and tail. The head-feathering is fine to the touch as moleskin, and of vel-

The Herald's Official Robe

vety blackness. He has full brilliant eyes, and a beak by which he can be identified. The mandibles are close the length of a duck's, but pointed and rather sharp, of a beautiful white, with opalescent tints of pale pink and salmon. The nostrils are long and sharply cut, and a narrow, rufous band bridges the upper part, lapping on each side of the lower. His make-up displays two unusual and comical attempts at decoration. At the base of the upper mandible the coot wears a large frontal plate of bright chestnut, and the under side of the short tail is lined with white. Aside from these, in his dark robe and black cowl he is in dress the plainest resident of the marsh.

During the breeding season the male bird lines off his nesting location and swims around close **Young** his mate, guarding, and keeping. her company. **Trum-** Woe to any bird that encroaches on the invisible **peters** boundary! Coots nest beside the water in the tall marsh grasses, and lay from six to ten large, yellowish-brown eggs, heavily dotted with darker spots on the larger end. The young, hatched after three weeks' brooding, take to the water as soon as their down is dry. In an unexpectedly short time they become self-supporting, and, with the addition of their baby chatter to the swelling volume of their elders', form a conspicuous feature of marsh music. No doubt your boat has shot past

THE HERALD OF DAWN

When the dawn's red glory tints the morning sky,
First the watchful Herald utters his wild cry,
Then all marsh birds answer that resounding, "Kew!"
While each tells the other, "I awakened you!"

The Music of the Marsh

small bays and screened pools often, and as the
chatter of old and young commingled in the music
of a coot party you have said, "That scarcely
sounds like ducks."

I have seen coots running throughout a season
in this swampy corner of a marsh, and it is as
nearly typical of their location as any I know. The
Indigo-
Bird's Nest
The muck of such places is alive with worms, the
grasses with insects, and the surrounding vines and
bushes bear seed. It seems that birds of any habit
might flourish there, and indeed I often have seen
a little red-eyed vireo so busy in these bushes that
I am sure there was a nest and family, and when
I landed and worked my way into the marsh I
scared up a female Indigo finch, and soon found
her nest in a thicket of blackberry and wild
grape.

Both were in bloom and growing so closely
around the little cup with its four delicate white
eggs that the brooding bird could have sat on her
nest and snapped up flies and gnats attracted by
the sweets of the flowers. The nest was securely
woven and placed in a perfect picture of loveliness,
the eggs appearing as pure and white as the berry
blooms, but I doubt if the brood came off safely.
That location was the most unfortunate I ever
knew an Indigo finch to choose. As I stood be-
side the nest I seemed to see big black water snakes,
weasels, coons, foxes, and a whole flock of bird

enemies stealing up to destroy it. I did not enter the thicket again, so its fate is unknown. But that a vireo and a finch should be homing in such a place proves how universally birds as well as flowers are distributed: Brilliant color attracts bird and insect musicians not only to the water's edge, but over it to the depth of the longest white water lily stem, which ranges from three feet to a specimen I once pulled that was sixteen.

The five typical flowers growing in the water at the outer edge of all other vegetation are the **Water** arrowhead lily, blue flag, yellow lily, water hya-**Flowers** cinth, white water lily, and differing members of their families. They are all beautiful plants of fine leaf and exquisite bloom; and there are some who will prefer one, and some another. My choice is the arrowhead, not only of marsh flowers. but among any; it ranks well toward first with me.

I love a red flower in the fields; it appears so vital, so full of life, it excites the imagination and warms the cockles of the heart; for red is love's own color. A red flower or fruit or leaf appears to be a consummation of something worth while; the fields have done a perfect work, now I must busy myself and produce results to prove what I am attempting. Any day my faith weakens. a bed of foxfire or cardinal flower waving salutation can renew my courage and urge me on with fresh zeal; and if a cardinal bird just then comes winging

THE FINCH COLOR SCHEME

Gold was the grape bloom, green the spray,
Nest and builder brownish gray,
Eggs and flowers pearly hue,
Master Musician indigo blue.

The Music of the Marsh

across my way, singing "Good cheer! Good cheer!"
I immediately feel so full of power that I dream
I can accomplish something worth doing.

Red is the love color, but white is the holy one;
and above all other white flowers the lily is em-
blematic of the holy of holies. Of all lilies not the
proud ascension nor the lowly lily of the valley is
so serenely, pearly pure as the arrowhead lifting
its jewels above the mire of the marsh. If only I
were a poet and had the gift of rhyming, or meas-
uring stately periods, I know the story well
enough. There are many things in nature that
bring the same thought to every heart. The com-
pilers of the Bible knew that when they epito-
mized the very Spirit of God in a dove and com-
pared the Prince of Peace with the white lily.
Above all else, white, unspotted white, is the em-
blem of truth, purity, and holiness; so this is the
song a poet should sing.

The lordly ascension lily was set high in the
fields as a perpetual reminder to men that Christ
gave His life, and ascended to heaven to inter-
cede for them with God the Father. The humble
lily of the valley was placed low among the grasses
of untraveled ways that any wanderer there might
see the emblem, so precious that it was said of
Jesus, "I am the lily of the valley." Then to the
muck and mire of the marsh the Almighty gave
the whitest and sweetest lily of all, that any lost and

sinking soul again might see with his latest vision the white sign of holiness.

There is music all the day among the rushes rustling with each breeze, and where they harp the purest note of God these white lilies grow. Their stems and buds are round, and the leaves wonderful. They are a fine arrow-shape, and some in this study were almost two feet in length, having a stout midrib, grooved on the upper surface, with deep veins on the under. Both bloom and leaf stems are round, and the bud is a perfect little globe, the sign of the earth. The lilies open with three simple petals that spread widely and curve with indescribable grace, so that light and shadow are caught on the face of the same bloom. No other white flower I know has the fineness of texture of the arrowhead petals; similar to pearls is the only comparison. Then they have a heart of gold, for the anthers are yellow, which adds richness to the petals.

Each stalk bears six clusters of bloom. The flowers are set on stems of sufficient length to display their beauty fully without crowding. Three blooms are placed at equal distances in a circle around the stem, and three inches above another circle, each stalk terminating in a cluster of four blooms: three around the stem, and one on the tip. The fragile, ethereal whiteness of the bloom is further enhanced by the surroundings. The back-

THE WHITE SIGN OF HOLINESS

The marshes were finished and gleaming
With crimson and purple, yellow and blue;
Then to prove them the work of the Master
He stamped the White Sign on them too.

The Music of the Marsh

ground is almost invariably graceful flowers, dark-green cattail leaves, and the golden-green, round, aspiring stems of the bulrush. These are genuine pointers; they are the signboards of earth directing man toward heaven. Water shallow enough to grow these lilies always shows the black muck of its bed, and this further emphasizes their appearance of purity. Worship is their due, and they receive it; for no mortal with senses alive to beauty can see them without having the joy song awakened in its most holy form in the heart.

Around them flit the sweet-lovers of the marsh with music-breeding wings, and in pursuit, equally musical, the dragon fly. At their feet the water folk are busy with the affairs of life, and among the lilies and between their slender stems dart the chattering grebes.

These small musicians can be shrill of voice and active with their bills in the fright of captivity; but at home in the marsh, filled with domestic **The Grebe's Lullaby** solicitude, they make their location charming with sweet, tender, low-voiced cheepings and chatter as they dart around, caring for their young. Grebe babies will thrill any normal human heart with tenderness. For a nest the mothers pull weeds from the marsh bed and stack them on a bit of morass, a grassy tuft, or drift-covered brush. They cover their eggs on leaving them, and when

389

the little ones are hatched their down is scarcely dry before they take to the water.

How cunning they are! Sitting like an auk, where you would expect a tail to be, yet it is not; tiny yellow feet, not webbed like a duck's, but the webbing in escallops on the outside of each flat toe; small, armlike wings; a bill that is sharp for a water bird; round, bright-irised eyes; plump, full breasts of finest snow-white velvet; backs striped much like those of young quail, and the baby not *larger than your thumb.*

On land they are the most helpless birds imaginable. They can not fly until almost fullgrown, and their legs are so far back they are unable to lift the weight of their bodies. They rise on their feet, launch themselves forward, with the tips of their wings breaking the fall on their breasts, and thus, like uncouth four-footed things, go sprawling until they reach the water.

One can see their comic relief and the deep breath they draw as they reach their native element. **Expert Swimmers** What a transformation! The prince of swimmers is the baby grebe. Like lightning play the tiny escalloped feet. It fairly seems to glide over the surface, not infrequently distancing its elders. When tired or ready to sleep these comical baby birds often climb upon the back of their mother, making a picture delightful to see.

The diving of the grown grebe is so nearly

THE LEAVES

"*Ye lispers, whisperers, singers in storms,*
Ye consciences murmuring faiths under forms,
Ye ministers meet for each passion that grieves,
Friendly, sisterly, sweetheart leaves,
As ye hang with your myriad palms upturned in the air,
Pray me a myriad prayer."   —*Lanier.*

The Music of the Marsh

without parallel that in many localities it is called the helldiver, on account of striking so deep and remaining so long that it is supposed to have ample time to reach the lower region and return before again seeing the surface. A grebe does dive deep and long; but do you understand the trick to which it resorts? Heading shoreward it comes up among driftwood or rushes, lifting above water just enough of the small, sharp bill to enable it to breathe, and with film-covered eyes and water-proof coat comfortably awaits the passing of danger, while pursuers are crediting it with wonderful ability in deep diving.

From babyhood the structural formation of the grebe remains unchanged. The wing feathers are almost spineless, and appear more like fringe than quills. Yet, being migratory, it must be able to make a strong flight. After reaching a chosen location, however, and beginning housekeeping, it will not take wing again until time to migrate. It will suffer itself to be picked up and killed before resorting to flight. For this reason it is the easiest prey imaginable for feather hunters.

A grebe very seldom leaves the water. When it does it propels the body with feet and wings, just as in young days, sits erect like an auk, or lies sunning in the same position taken in swimming. It is a rare thing to catch a grebe attempting to bear the weight of its body on the feet. The attitude assumed in so doing is distinctive, and not at all like the position taken by a duck or goose in standing. The breast is lifted so high there appears to be imminent danger of toppling backward.

The color is some shade of brown over the back, and whether you know what it is or not, you Grebe are familiar with the breast of the grebe. When Millinery you see a woman with a band of white plumage tinted almost invisibly with blue and green, and more strongly with golden brown, ornamenting her hat, know that from one to six of these harmless, lovable, sweet-voiced birds were stripped from chin to vent to supply it. When you see that other woman wearing a cape, the collar of which reaches above her ears and the skirt to her elbows, and it is made of almost indiscernible, delicately-colored sections the size of your hand, know that each stands for the life of one of these charming marsh chatterers.

The breast of the grebe is its curse. The feathers are so tiny and fine as to render adequate description impossible. There are eight members of the family having this exquisite plumage, that varies in rarity with the different species. Crested grebes are killed without mercy for this small patch of rare feathering, and their marsh cousins do not escape. There is no bird slaughter for plumage more wanton, unless it be that practiced by the

394

THE HELL-DIVER

"I am a Grebe, as any one easily can see,
But I'm badly abused,
And my right name ain't used,
Because I'm such a deep-diver," says he.

The Music of the Marsh

egret hunters, who take the life of the brooding bird for a few beautiful feathers found on the shoulders only at nesting-time, and leave the young to slow death from starvation.

When plume-decked women chide you for taking a moderate amount of game in season, tell them this egret story. Tell them, too, how the grebes are caught by hand, because they will not fly; and how the skin of the throat is cut with nippers and ripped to the vent of the living bird, which is then left to die as it may in its chosen location among the grasses, rushes, and blue flags of the marsh border.

Here is a cloying sweetness that insures an unusually strong insect chorus, attracted first to the blue flags. These flowers, borne singly upon slender, upright stems, are of complicated arrangement in their hearts, so they were given a far-reaching sweetness that many visitors might be lured to them and thus accomplish their cross-fertilization. They have three curving, graceful petals curling back, of many tinted purplish shades; three upright pale-blue ones inside them, much smaller in size, and a complicated arrangement of pistil and fringy anthers in their hearts, that touches the bloom with gold. These anthers are designed especially to catch the pollen of their kind, carried on the backs of bees, so that, even if the plants can not reach each other, their species is perpetu-

397

Music of the Wild

ated. These complex parts in the hearts of flowers are their sex organism, and the honey they distil is the bribe offered bees and butterflies to consummate conception for them. Nature is very frank, and these marvels are spread closely over her face for any one who cares to learn. I think those who really understand and appreciate these delicate processes among the flowers never again doubt that there is a Supreme Being. The Creator said, "And a bow shall be set in the cloud; and I will look upon it, that I may remember the everlasting covenant between God and every living creature of all flesh that is upon the earth." So He evolved the rainbow. On the painted lily faces the botanists of early Greece saw reproduced these wonderful colors, and so they named the plant "Ιρις,"—the rainbow.

Because the sky is blue, eternal, and never-changing, men have adopted this color to express True Blue friendship, which also should be eternal and never-changing. True blue is dear to all hearts and conveys an express meaning; so again these wonderful flowers are baptized with truth. And as if no honor might be lacking, to the blue is added "flag." Never was other flower more highly honored in its naming. Sometimes beautiful plants and vines are insulted by scientists applying to them careless, contradictory, and incongruous terms. Here is one embarrassed by riches both in its scientific and

398

THE BLUE FLAG

"The god that dwells among the reeds
Sang sweetly from their tangled bredes;
The soft-tongued water murmured low,
Swinging the flag-leaves to and fro."
—Thompson.

The Music of the Marsh

common name. Think what his flag symbolizes to a man! It means so much that for it he severs the dearest ties of earth, leaves a home of comfort and faces untold hardships, exposes his body to sickness, wounds, and many forms of death. For it he sacrifices everything else on earth, yielding with smiling lips life itself.

So when the slender, exquisite leaves of the iris waved on the free winds of the marsh with the abandon and grace of a flag, some one caught the resemblance, and to the symbol of eternal truth was added that of liberty, and the rainbow lily became the blue flag, the true flag.

It is not alone in complicated arrangement of parts to facilitate cross-fertilization. Many marsh and swamp flowers have similar hearts, with much sweetness as a lure, so that not only wild bees and insects but many butterflies are constant visitors.

Although this study was made on a roadside flower, the black swallow-tail is a true marsh butterfly and beautiful above all others. The wing- A Butterfly sweep is from three and a half to four inches, and Aristocrat this is one of the few aristocrats of butterflydom, because it bears trailed wings. These wings are black above, with lines of yellow spots running across them. They are lemon-yellow below, with the row of spots showing through. The trailers are black, touched with a stroke of strong yellow, and the upper sides of the back pair of wings each have a spot of blue. In company with Troilus, Archippus, and Cœnia, these handsomest of all marsh butterflies flutter slowly from flower to flower, providing most beautiful pictures where everything is·a component part of one great, brilliant panorama.

What a quantity of gold there is in a marsh when it even takes wing and flies through the air! **Pure Gold** So many of the plants and flowers are yellow that in August the color predominates all around the borders; yes, and even more. It lifts above the water as well; for there is the yellow lily, the purest gold of all, sturdily erecting its unalloyed head above the murky surface.

Its habitat is a short distance farther out than the arrowhead lily and the blue flag. It requires more water. The white pond lily leaf and bloom rests directly on the surface, the yellow raises its thick, woolly leaf and flower stems above. The blooms have six cuppy, deeply overlapping petals of purest gold at the tip, green at the base outside, and maroon of bright color inside. In the smallest species the inside maroon is almost red. The stigma is a deep yellow disk, very large; and as it ripens the stamens seem to peel from it and grow dusty with pollen, while the flower unfolds.

On the first day of bloom the petals open so narrowly that any bee entering must of necessity trail the pollen adhering to its fuzz, across the

FLYING GOLD

"As poised on vibrant wings,
Where its sweet treasure swings
The honey-lover clings

The Music of the Marsh

stigma. When the bloom petals fall the disk grows rapidly into a large head with the appearance of having a lid. This pod is full of seed, that the Indians grind for one of their dainties at wedding feasts. These balls of gold, before they are fully open, resemble small fallen suns; and when we reflect that the sun stands for light and warmth, by which we live, yellow becomes our most precious color. There is not so much sound on the yellow lilies as on the white or blue, but there is a world of busy musicians all around them.

A tea party of prima donnas would not reveal sweeter tones than the incessant vocalizing of a flock of wild ducks. They make entrancing music. At one moment come notes of glad content over motherhood, sunshine, and feasting; then an endearing call as they gather small ones close to them; then a warning lest a venturesome baby stray too far; then a word of satisfaction over a very luscious worm, and too often the high alarm cry when the water riffles with a big turtle or muskrat coming their way. When a rival interferes with his love-making, a courting drake sends across the marsh a hair-raising scream, quite unlike that of his domesticated cousin. **The Original Quack**

The marsh music of wild geese is almost of the same character, differing from the ducks only in tone and one tribal call. The "Honk! Honk!" of the old gander that leads his wedge-shaped flock

Music of the Wild

in migration is a distinctive note, but it gives small idea of the vocal power he displays when he marshals his followers on the lakes and rivers of Canada.

"Couk, conk, conk!" The cry of the sheitpoke is composed of enlivening notes, and rings with the The Cry of the Sheitpoke delight of boundless freedom. Coming unexpectedly, it is, to say the least, startling. The sheitpoke is of the heron family, and he is a bird that deserves sympathetic admiration,—he attends his own affairs so diligently and appears so absorbed in them. He goes about his business in such a "hammer and tongs" style that the heart warms to his independence. Rolling his jolly call, he comes slashing and splashing through muck and water, quite as frequently for mischief as in search of food—the veriest rowdy in the marsh. Soiled and dripping, he reaches a solid footing with a look half apologetic, half defiant, exactly as if he were saying, "Had a lot of fun doing that; but why in the world do you suppose I did it?"

He is a warm-hearted, warm-headed, impulsive roustabout, yet at the first suspicious note introduced into his paradise he can slink like a cuckoo. His generous crest flattens until it appears pasted down; his oily, hairlike plumage hugs his body, and his eyes snap and pop. A frightened sheitpoke trying to decide in which direction to flee an unknown danger is an amusing spectacle. He is

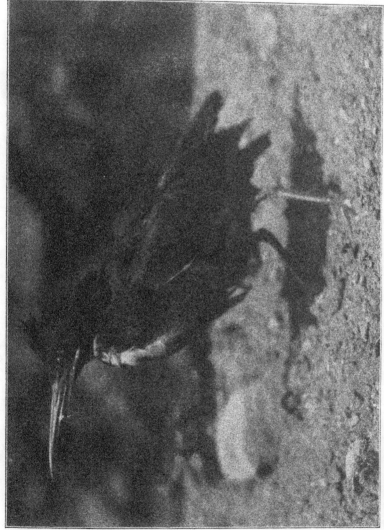

THE MARSH ROWDY

"My heart was just completely broke
When some one went and named me 'Sheitpoke,'
So I'll roll my britches above my knees,
And romp through the marshes as I please."

The Music of the Marsh

not an extremely handsome bird. An old male has
a few beautiful iridescent feathers around the back
of the neck and across the shoulders, the throat is
narrowly striped with cream; but the general color
is a dark, dull brown. He has smooth, scaled legs
and feet of greenish yellow, full bright eyes, and
quite a lively coloring on his elegantly shaped bill.
He is a romping, mischievous, free, wild bird, and
no marsh choir would be complete without his clear,
ringing notes.

If it be fair to laugh at anything that is young
and helpless, then a baby sheitpoke is almost, if
not quite, the most laughable specimen in birdland.
A long, slender, yellow-tinted beak; long, slender
neck; long, slender legs; long, slender body; big,
popping eyes; an insatiable appetite, and vocal
powers to proclaim it loudly around the marsh.

Of the same location as the yellow lily are the
water hyacinths. Their leaves lift above the sur-
face, are near one-fourth the size of the yellow lily, Water
and lance-shaped. They are a crisp dark-green Hyacinths
and stiffly upstanding. The stems of the leaf and
bloom are very similar to the yellow lily, except
that the blooms rise on an average of six or eight
inches higher and are a long head set with tiny
bracts, in each of which blooms an exquisite little
blue flower. Blooming begins at the base and
slowly climbs to the tip, the lower flowers fading
before the top are all open. The head is of pure

409

Music of the Wild

blue and forms a rare and graceful addition to marsh flowers. I mean rare in the sense of rarely beautiful. The entire plant is artistic. It attracts bees and insects for its music; the waves come lipping around it, and birds that hunt food near are the feathered giants of the marsh, the real operatic high C singers—the bittern, loon, and blue heron.

When the bittern booms, when the loon cries, when the blue heron screams, you hear the Calvés and the Melbas of the marsh; but you must decide for yourself to which belongs the palm. The bittern and heron are of the same family. The bittern is plumper of body, shorter of beak and leg, with a handsome golden-brown back. A black line begins at each corner of the mouth, passes under the eye, and gradually widens until it meets the corresponding line at the back of the neck. The breast is of creamy white, beautifully outlined in shaded stripes of golden brown. . Excepting the white heron, a bird of snow and surpassingly beautiful, the breast of the bittern is the most exquisite piece of feather-marking in the entire heron family. These birds nest on the ground, and their bony, long-billed babies are very interesting.

Scientists are yet discussing whether the bittern really booms. Actual contact with the birds, instead of research in ancient authorities, would settle many a similar vexing question. Surely the bittern booms. Go live in the haunts of one long

Marsh Prima Donnas [side note]

When the Bittern Booms [side note]

410

WATER HYACINTHS

As the faintest murmur, at the lilies feet,
Break the rolling wavelets, in their rhythmic beat.
Heart-shaped leaves uplifted, heads of azure blue,
What the waters tell them,—if I only knew!

The Music of the Marsh

enough to become sufficiently familiar to photograph him, and by that time you will have learned for yourself. You also will find that his boom does closely resemble the low, distant rumble of an angry bull, and that, although partly nocturnal when breeding, and frequently throughout the entire season, he sometimes booms during the day, and is in evidence while bathing and fishing. We gravely are told by more than one old-school ornithologist that he feeds only at night and booms only during the breeding season, always under cover of darkness. If he could not be heard frequently around the marsh during the summer, and pictured as he feeds at almost any hour of the day, this might be given credence. In fact hunters and fishers sometimes remark, "We must look out for a bull," when it is the rumbling "Umm-umm-umm" of the bittern they hear.

It is on account of this boom that in backwood localities he is called the "thunder-pumper." The boom supplies the "thunder." The "pumper" **The Thunder Pumper** arises from the fact that he is supposed to have an extra intestine running straight through his anatomy; he thrusts his beak into a small puddle he wishes to explore for worms, and with a "ca-chook! ca-chook!" pumps off the water and feasts at his leisure. There are places where this belief is so firm that it would be unwise to appear to think it amusing. The only method by which to convince any one of its untruth would be to dissect a bird and find the peculiar membrane in his windpipe that enables him to furnish this distinctive and most interesting marsh music. No doubt the organ would somewhat resemble the same formation at the base of the windpipe of a drake.

The bittern is a fine, dignified specimen. He likes to have his beak and feet clean, and manifests his pride in his beautiful plumage by constantly dressing and keeping it immaculate. Compared with his cousin, shielpoke, he differs as the prince from the fishmonger. No slashing and splashing in marsh muck and dirty water for him. He selects a clear, clean spot having a slight current and, standing immovable, watches the bottom until he sees signs of a worm; and then, with a quick, neat nip he has it.′ He is in every way a self-respecting bird. He moves with fine poise and dignity, and in flight he is strong and graceful. His vocalizing is almost as surprising as that of the loon, but quite different.

The loon is a diver, and a relative of the grebe. As a rule loons are of the lakes and marshes of the **The** far North, where their cries are considered dread**Laughter** ful by nervous people. In early spring, near nest**of the Loon** ing-time, their vocalization is startling, especially in a first experience. The morning call rolling across the water is not so unpleasant; some eminent authorities confess a sneaking fondness for it, as

WHERE THE LOON LAUGHS "'T is only God may be had for the asking;
There is no price set on the lavish summer,
And June may be had by the poorest comer."
—Lowell.

The Music of the Marsh

if it were a thing for which to apologize. Perhaps they hesitate to admit it on account of the mournful evening and night cry, which is a terror, resembling a rolling, melancholy, long-drawn "Ha, ha! week! Ha, ha! week." Poets have written of the laughing of the loon; but as this cry swells across the marsh, gathering force as it travels, until it comes reverberating from the forests and hills of the distance, it seems to awaken feelings similar to those roused by the cries of a hungry panther. As loons occur only as straying migrants in my country, I am not sufficiently acquainted with them to know what act accompanies these cries, or why they are uttered. It is presumable that the loon is having just as good a time as any other bird, and no doubt his crazy laughter is uttered in calling a mate, in love-making, or to express the pure enjoyment of his life.

After an experience with loon music it is almost a relief to hear the rasping scream of a blue heron—"Ker-awk! ker-awk!" The entire family of cranes and herons are beautiful marsh birds. The blue heron is a fine specimen, at times over forty inches in height, with an immense beak; bright, steel-blue plumage, clearly marked with black, brown, and white; high crest, flowing beard, eyes that snap as the bird vaguely realizes an unseen danger, and feathers sparkling with mist and dew from the wet rushes among which he feeds.

Music of the Wild

The Battle-cry of the Heron A heron's voice is at its best when he calls his mate; but even then those who all their lives have studied bird notes under stress of different emotions have difficulty in deciding whether he says, "Come, my love; this spot is propitious. Share a morning treat with your dearest!" or, "Better keep away, old skin and bones; there's danger around this frog pond!" But what he says when he defends his mate and young from intruders there is no trouble in understanding, and he emphasizes it with beak, wings, and feet. That is the hoarse, rasping battle-cry of the heron, and if you do not want to fight you had better run.

The Drum-Majors of the Marsh Water carries sound so clearly and for such distances the woodpeckers and flickers that choose marsh drums for their performances outdo their fellow musicians of the land. Every hollow, vine-covered tree stump of the marsh is a big bassdrum, and on it these drummers perform all day with never-ending vigor, while the breast of the water serves as their sounding-board. When they have drummed until they are tired clinging to their instruments, they lean back and cry, "Kerr, kerr, kerr!" like the wailing notes of a fife, and then return to their drumming.

To these performers of the day and partly of the night now are added other musicians, wholly nocturnal, that have arrived from the forest. When dusk creeps from the deep wood and in-

418

THE DRUM-MAJOR

He wears a modest uniform
Of gray, with black and white,
He plays the   e till short o breath

The Music of the Marsh

closes the marsh there is short time for pause be-
fore the singers of darkness lift their voices. The
frogs begin with renewed energy. Before the The
Sere-
naders
moon silvers the water and blackens the shadows
comes the whip-poor-will's cry. It is not unmu-
sical, but it comprises peculiar notes; they are
enunciated so clearly. and with such insistence, and
mingled always with the mystery of the dark. Not
mystery because the moon looks on anything
different from the sun, but because we are in
darkness; and when we hear and can not see,
we dread.

Near the same time the night jar lifts his
voice, and he is a veritable screamer. What a cry
he can utter! We shudder involuntarily. But
what of the mate he calls? Did you ever pause
to think that to her perhaps the cry means:
"Awake! Come, sail with me through the forest
and over the marsh! Let us search for food
and enjoy life!" Is there not more in that to
arouse sympathy than repulsion in the human
heart?

The maestro of all night musicians is the great
horned owl. The big hollow sycamores and the im-
penetrable thickets around the marsh are his birth-
right. His music echoes throughout the year and
belongs to his location as the white mantle of win-
ter and the green of summer. It is not that his
cry is harsh or unmusical, but that coupled with

Music of the Wild

darkness his notes are so startling. If a belated
hunter was not acquainted with the bird when the
deep-toned "Who, huh, whoo, who, waugh?" comes
rolling out of the darkness, he well might wonder
whether his imperative questioner used the voice
of bird, beast, or devil.

It is the marsh that furnishes the croakings,
the chatter, the quackings, the thunder, the cries,
The Choral Union and the screams of birdland. These notes may
seem disagreeable as they are described, but they
are not so in realization. At times we may think
that we would be glad not to hear again the most
discordant of these musicians, but they are all dear
in their places, and were any one of them to be-
come extinct, something of its charm would be
taken from the damp, dark, weird marsh life that
calls us so strongly. We have learned to know
and understand them, and they have won our sym-
pathy and our love. We would miss the strident
rasp, the flapping of wings, and the vision of
long-legged awkwardness as they rise from the
rushes; for these are prominent parts of the at-
tractions we go to seek.

As the season advances the choir of the marsh
is augmented, not only by the natural increase of
its true residents, but also by swarms of birds lov-
ing the water, seeds, and insects afforded; and the
moment they are free from other duties they come
flocking here with their young. In early August

The Music of the Marsh

the rushes are weighted with bobolinks, and the air resounds with their sweet, liquid notes. A few days later the straying killdeer and upland plover return, and the blackbirds and tanagers sweep upon it in countless numbers. From then until fall migration marsh life is at its fullest and best, and if from its babel of voices comes an occasional rasping note, to counteract it there is an endless variety of exquisite tones to the heart of the music-lover most dear.

To any man the call of the marsh is threefold. Whether he realizes it or no, his faith in all renewal is strengthened in watching this yearly resurrection. Dead as any death appears the marsh during winter's long sleep; no other place so abundant with life in summer. Most people dread the thought of annihilation. The marsh, that can die and yet return to life at the first breath of spring, seems each year to repeat anew to its lovers, "Though a man die, yet shall he live again." All men are cheered by that message, whether it comes by precept or impression.

There is a visual call from the marsh. Men travel across continents and pay high prices to purchase the greatest reproductions of nature that have been painted. The marsh is the most wonderful picture nature herself has to offer. There is no sky to surpass these, for all skies drift over in answer to changing moods. There are no clouds

The Three-fold Lure of the Marsh

Music of the Wild

so real as these, that are reality. There is no
background so perfect as giants of the forest de-
veloping from the beginning; no middle distance
so beautiful as these plumes of wild rice sweeping
the sky, these waving flags and rushes, this riot of
red and yellow, white and blue flower faces; no
foreground so rare as this mass of growing leaves
and lily pads that shade off into the black, un-
fathomable water. There is no still life to sur-
pass in grandeur the upheavals of nature in a tem-
pest. There are no subjects more picturesque than
stilt-legged waders that stand motionless by the
hour or rise on wide wings and with trailing legs
make nature's picture complete by sailing slowly
across it. And the breath of muck-ladened air,
touched with the resin of pines, heavy with the
perfume of pollen, pungent with the tang of
mint,—this is atmosphere for hunger of which
the nostrils may wither; but whose brush shall re-
produce it?

Always there is the call of the music; the best
in the wide world, the spontaneous, day long, night
long song of freedom and content. From a mil-
lion gauze-winged musicians, from the entire
aquatic orchestra singing to the accompaniment of
the pattering rain, from the killdeer's call trailing
across the silver night, from the coot waking the
red morning, from the chattering blackbirds of
golden noon, from the somber-robed performers of

WHERE MARSH AND FOREST MEET

Night was born in deep forest,
  In the heart of its secret place,
Slowly she creeps to the marshland,
  And veils her glowing face.

The Music of the Marsh

the gray evening,—comes the great call that above all others lures men to return again, and yet again, to revel in it; comes the sweetest note from the voice of the wild; comes the music of the marsh.

CPSIA information can be obtained
at www.ICGtesting.com
Printed in the USA
LVHW01s2325120618
580568LV00010B/312/P